# CITY CHILDREN, COUNTRY SUMMER

# CITY CHILDREN, COUNTRY SUMMER

Lawrence Wright

CHARLES SCRIBNER'S SONS / NEW YORK

Copyright © 1979 Lawrence Wright

Library of Congress Cataloging in Publication Data:

Wright, Lawrence (date).
  City children, country summer.

  1. Fresh air charity-Pennsylvania. I. Title.

HV936.P4W⁻4    362.⁷′1    ⁻9-1348
ISBN 0-684-16144-3

1 3 5 7 9 11 13 15 1⁻ 19 O/C 20 18 16 14 12 10 8 6 4 2

Printed in the United States of America

Grateful acknowledgment is made to quote the following copyrighted
material: "Every page Rich with humor," by permission of Harvey
Features ® Richie Rich © Harvey Features; parody of "Rudolph the
Red-Nosed Reindeer," copyright © 1949 St. Nicholas Music, Inc.,
renewed 197⁻, by permission of St. Nicholas Music, Inc.; "Come on,
come on! Have a Pepsi Day!", by permission of the copyright and
trademark owner © Pepsico, Inc. 1976; quotations with reference to
Captain America, copyright © 19⁻7 Marvel Comics Group, a Division of Cadence Industries Corp., all rights reserved, by permission
of Marvel Comics Group; lines from and new version of "Hot Line,"
by permission of Perren-Vibes Music Inc./Bull Pen Music Inc.: "We
do it all for you" ® by permission of McDonald's Corporation.

# ACKNOWLEDGMENTS

This book owes many debts of time and spirit which I am grateful to acknowledge, beginning with the officers and associates of the Fresh Air Fund; Ann Kanagy, the Fund's representative in the Kishacoquillas Valley; and then, of course, the parents in both New York and Pennsylvania, who trusted me to explore the special lives of their children. Additional thanks go to Laurie Graham, who conceived the book and edited it with taste and imagination; to Professor John A. Hostetler, who checked the accuracy of my observations of Amish and Mennonite life; and to my wife, Roberta, as keen a reporter as I have ever worked with. Finally, I want to express my fullest thanks to the children who adopted us into their summer, and to whom this book is affectionately, and admiringly, dedicated.

# PRINCIPAL CHARACTERS

| CITY CHILDREN | COUNTRY HOSTS |
|---|---|
| Natasha Brown | Dorcas Swarey |
| Eddie Cato | Ivan and Aire Stoltzfus |
| Tyrone Howard | Kore and Esther Peachey, Galen and Janet |
| Darrell (D.J.) Jackson | Norman and Martha Kanagy, and Darrell (Drill) |
| Macy Mizell | Daniel and Ruth Byler, Anna Louise, Rose, Elmer, Samuel, Timmy, and Myron |
| Donny Perez | Alphie and Rachel Kauffman, and Glenn |
| Julio Ruiz | Fred and Effie Peachey |
| Franklin Williams | Aquilla and Ann Peachey, and Luke |

# CITY CHILDREN,
## COUNTRY SUMMER

# Macy's Dream

"When I was there they had a sliding board. It was a real long one but if you slide a certain way you go into this deep pool—it was never-ending. One time we had just finished dinner and the dishes and after that everybody was doing their usual thing, the mother was sewing clothes. Anna Louise and Rose said let's go out on the porch and there was this sliding board. It was like on the porch all the way down to where the garden is, only the pool was in the grass.

"I was sliding and all of a sudden somebody was in front of me, and you know those poor skinny people that ain't get nothin' to eat or ain't get no clothes or anything? Like this picture I saw on TV these people were all rolled up in balls. I got scared. I just stopped, and when she got off I slipped on down to the part where the deep pool was and I swam across to the other side, and everywhere I saw these poor people, ten and eleven years old. I thought maybe they had some disease or sump'm. I axed Rose Byler did they usually come around? And she said yeah, 'cause they feed them and their mother Ruth was making some clothes for them to put on. I woke up 'cause I heard my sister and my uncle talking and I was trying to go back to sleep.

"To me, it means that they were helping the poor, instead of letting them die in the road."

# Chapter 1

The Kishacoquillas Valley lies midway between Johnstown and Harrisburg in the deep furrows of the Pennsylvania ridge country. It is formed by two sinuous mountains in the Allegheny chain which run on a north-northeast slant and close together at both ends. The result is a geological oddity known as an isolated valley, meaning that it has no visible entrance. The valley has always been a natural sanctuary, first for Indians, then for white settlers who jostled their wagons up the whitewater rapids of Kishacoquillas Creek; and even now the encircling mountains are a reef against the wash of news, fashion, tourism, and television on which the tide of American civilization advances. The Amish and Mennonite farmers who live in the valley today think of themselves as God's colony on earth. They believe that the beauty of the land should be enhanced by the beauty of their own labor, because a world freed of ugliness and idleness may more fully be freed of sin. The Shawnee name, Kishacoquillas, means "The snakes are already in their dens."

A castaway from the Interstate highways, who landed by chance on State Road 655, would find the usual adjuncts of his travel changed or absent. The signal on his radio would grow dim and scratchy. The billboards which have sharpened his appetite for food, gas, or accommodations would give way to passages of scripture, starkly white on black, standing rigidly above the luxuriant cornfields; or to hand-painted admonitions against Sunday fishing in the limestone creekbeds; or to foreboding non sequiturs—CARS AREN'T ALL THE MAKER RECALLS—which hint of punishment and spiritual disquiet.

If the castaway stopped to chat he would find little in common with the average roadside informant—unless perhaps he were a castaway meteorologist, and the vagaries of weather in every nuance were important to him. The informant may never have heard of Warren Burger, Norman Mailer, or Farrah Fawcett-Majors; he may not be able to name more than five elected government officials at any level, including the President of the United States and the Governor of Pennsylvania. The reference points the castaway brings with him—the books he's read, the places he's been, the variety of people he's known—aren't likely to impress the provincial mind, which believes that sophistication is evil. Even the data that the castaway carries around in his head, which make him a full-fledged member of the media culture—election returns, baseball scores, Supreme Court decisions— would be dully received in the valley, unless they add fuel to opinions already strongly held. A conversation about current events in the Middle East may be met with the news that the Chinese militia is preparing to cross the Euphrates, and vultures are multiplying in Israel for the feast of Armageddon. The castaway is likely to leave the valley with the impression that his informant has a head full of nonsense; and yet, when the informant closes his eyes the world does not whir in front of him, and his mind does not fill at once with jingles and commercial advertisements. His world is so familiar to him that it cannot be shut out. He can turn in every direction and see each detail as clearly as if his eyes were open. He does not have to look up to know that the sky is full of sun and swallows. He can cover his ears and hear the wind running through the crops and livestock tearing the grass.

Like the water in the valley, which flows in both directions, the people who live there follow their own formulas, irrespective of universal axioms. The sun rises over Jacks Mountain and sets over Stone Mountain, but despite this empirical evidence natives point to Stone Mountain and call it north; and to the north end of State Road 655, which bisects the valley, and call it east. Directions for the traveler who stops to ask aren't likely to be helpful until he's adjusted to the valley's compass.

Time is a matter of opinion. Most Mennonites in the valley keep their clocks five to ten minutes fast, even though they are never in a hurry, and more conservative believers will run from twenty minutes to an hour fast. The more advanced a person's clock, it seems, the further back in historical time he chooses to live in terms of dress, attitudes, and manner of living. The Amish like to stay half an hour ahead, but since they don't observe daylight saving time they run half an hour slow in summer. The lunch whistle at the Allensville Planing Mill blows exactly at noon; ask a local what time it is when the whistle sounds and you can make a fair guess what church he belongs to by the answer he gives.

It is a brittle society. Big Valley, as the Kishacoquillas Valley is usually called, is famous among anthropologists for having the largest number of cleavages of any Amish-Mennonite community in the United States. "Progress" is the fulcrum on which it balances, or breaks. A farmer who plows with the latest John Deere tractor and milks his cows electrically may live next to a man who lights his home with kerosene, tills his land behind a team of Belgian horses, and crops his lawn with a staked goat. It is as if all the strata of an archaeological site came to life simultaneously.

The people who live in the valley view the many divisions in the Amish and Mennonite churches as rungs on a ladder that stretches from the "lowest," or most conservative Old Order Amish (the horse-and-buggy types), to the more liberal, or "higher" Mennonite groups. Nearly every aspect of one's appearance or dress is subordinated in some way to the strictures of one's place on this ladder, including the length of hair, the width of a hat brim, the fabric in a dress. A church in transition is instantly signaled by modifications of these strictures. On the middle rung of the ladder, between the buggy Amish and the Mennonites, stand the Beachy Amish, who drive cars and use telephones and electricity. Some of the Beachy men taper their hair in back, instead of cutting it bluntly, and abbreviate the full-length Solzhenitsyn beards (mustaches are forbidden because of their "military" connotations) into trim goatees.

The most visible index of progressiveness is the devotional covering, the lace cap which symbolizes the woman's dependency on her father or husband. Among the Old Order Amish the covering is a full white bonnet; for Mennonites, the covering shrinks from one congregation to another—or, within a congregation, from one generation to another—until it is sometimes called a "cupcake," and is worn only in church. Some women have given it up entirely. These changes, when they occur, are read instantly by the whole community, and may cause years of commentary about what will happen next. Next they'll be wearing belts instead of suspenders; next they'll wear bright clothing; next their women will wear makeup and jewelry; next they'll be drinking and divorcing and acting like Presbyterians. As one climbs the ladder toward higher congregations of Mennonites, these gradations are gradually achieved.

The Old Order Amish in Big Valley are split conspicuously among white-top buggies, yellow-top buggies, and black buggies, and there are further divisions within these groups. The yellow-tops and the white-tops broke apart in 1849, and besides the color of their buggies (and the fact that they ride on rubber wheels, rather than iron rims) yellow-toppers define themselves by wearing a single suspender, Li'l Abner style, and women wear brown bonnets. They are called "bean-soupers," because of their usual menu after Sunday preaching. Like the black-buggy Amish, they may use color in their fabrics, and their favorite shades are mauve, violet, teal blue, and turquoise.

White-toppers are the least assimilated into the "English" way of life, as the Amish call the non-Amish; locally white-toppers are known as Nebraskas, because nearly a century ago they had a bishop from that state. Nebraskas are a curiosity even to other Amishmen, who admire their intransigence but at the same time think of them as dirty and rough—the community Snopeses. They live off by themselves in unkempt and unpainted houses—secluded even from the cloistered society of Big Valley—in a style not much different from that of the frontier homesteaders before the Industrial Revolution. The men wear their hair to their shoulders and let their beards go untrimmed; they dress in white shirts and brown trousers with no belts or suspenders (pants are laced up in back), and their broad straw hats have the widest brims in the valley. Their wives wear plain, dark dresses that reach nearly to the ground; over their devotional covering they wear a black kerchief, and over that a straw hat with the brim tied down over the ears. On market day, when Nebraskas come to town, the men affect a kind of nervous swagger, like rustics in the city, and children cling to their parents as if contagion might sweep them away.

Nebraskas forbid any adornment of the home, including window shades, screens, rugs, pictures, or even projecting eaves. All modern conveniences are taboo. The white-buggies bisected in 1942, when one of their members purchased an English farm and refused to saw the eaves from his buildings. Actually, the split wasn't accomplished until another white-topper, in a teasing gesture of sympathy, built a doghouse with a projecting roof.

Cleavage is the only way the social system of the valley can allow for religious or cultural diversity. "This system of stratification permits the person to move gradually from a 'lower' group to a more progressive one in a natural and slow manner," writes John A. Hostetler in *Amish Society* (Dr. Hostetler, a professor of anthropology and sociology at Temple University, is a native of the Kishacoquillas Valley). "The boundaries of each religious community are preserved by excommunication of the deviant person: he simply moves up the ladder to a 'higher' church and in this way establishes adjustment without 'contaminating' his own kin."

The most recent division in the valley is unusual in that it merged two dissenting factions from the yellow-top and the black-buggy churches. The principal issue was a matter of theology: whether or not one can be assured of salvation. The Amish believe that no one can know that he is going to be saved, he can only hope for the best. So when members of the two churches began to believe that one could be assured of salvation, they had the choice of joining a Mennonite congregation or forming their own church. Both choices involved excommunication from their previous churches and being shunned by many relatives and old friends. The inflexibility of Amish society requires that these breaks be sharp and painful.

When a sect breaks off, as this one did, there is often a period of accommodation with technology—an uncomfortable time for the members of the new church, because they are flirting with taboos they have avoided all their lives. Some of the younger members from the yellow-top contingent already owned tractors, which they used for belt power in their barns, and although they still avoid using the tractors in the fields they sometimes drive around the neighborhood just to get the feel of motorized transport. A few families in the new sect have rationalized the need for a telephone in connection with their farm work—to call the vet in an emergency, or to place an order that would save a trip into town—so they have phones put in their barns. These barn phones come with extraordinarily loud signals so that their ring can be heard in the house. When a friend calls, he knows to let it ring and ring and ring in order for the party on the other end to jump up from the table or out of bed, put on his shoes, light a lantern if it's dark, negotiate the snow or ice or barnyard droppings, calm the panic in the stable caused by the alarming noise, and finally answer the phone.

Virtually all of the Mennonites in the valley came from the Amish church at some point in their ancestry, if not in their own lifetimes. The two religions have a sibling relationship which goes back to the Swiss Anabaptist movement of the sixteenth century—a radical experiment because it took literally the lessons of the Sermon on the Mount, in which Jesus communicated the principles of the first church. The Anabaptists renounced oaths and revelry, and advocated non-resistance, both in battle and in court. They accepted Martin Luther's Reformation, but spurned the doctrine of infant baptism and a state church. They also believed in dressing plainly, so that, in the words of Menno Simons, the Dutch priest after whom the Mennonites took their name, "not the outward adorning of the body but the inward adorning of the spirit is desired and sought with great zeal and diligence, with a broken heart and a contrite mind." The movement spread so quickly in central Europe that it threatened state control of the church, and as a result the Anabaptists were persecuted by the Catholic hierarchy and, within the Reformation, by the Protestants. In the first ten years of the Anabaptist movement over five thousand members were drowned, burned, crucified, buried alive, or otherwise eliminated. The sect was nearly exterminated in Switzerland by "Mennonite hunters," who arrested all believers over the age of sixteen, to be exiled or sold as galley slaves to the Italian navies.

In the late seventeenth century an elder named Jacob Amman, a strident and uncompromising leader, forced a split in the Mennonite church over the issue of *Meidung,* or shunning, which he thought should be strictly enforced against excommunicated members. He also urged a more severe attitude toward dress, and renounced buttons as a military influence. Thus the Mennonites were called *Knöpler* (buttoners), and the followers of Jacob Amman were known as *Häftler* (hooks-and-eyers). Later, of course, the Amish were called by the name of their founder.

Both the Amish and the Mennonites accepted William Penn's invitation to settle in his colony, the "holy experiment" of Pennsylvania, although as much as possible they emigrated on separate boats and tried to keep some

distance from each other's settlements. The Amish settled first in Berks and Lancaster counties, which were still
troubled by Indian raids. When they heard of the natural
defense of the hidden valley of Kishacoquillas, many
sought sanctuary there (the first Amishman to take out a
deed in the valley was Christian Zook, in 1792). They
found the valley already occupied by Scotch-Irish Presbyterians. Fifty years later the Scotch-Irish had for the
most part been bought out and pushed aside; today the
Presbyterians congregate in the towns or in the "tight
end" of the valley, the narrow and rocky hollow to the
south.

Family names such as Yoder, Peachey, Byler, Kanagy, Zook, original Amish settlers, are so common in the
valley that they have almost dropped from general use.
If Earl A. Yoder and his family are coming to dinner (the
noon meal), one doesn't say the Yoders are coming; one
says the Earl A.'s are coming. Where the first name and
middle initial fail to define the head of the household, he
is referred to by the name of his father, his father's father,
and on up the male line until this particular Earl Yoder
is satisfactorily singled out: e.g., Sims-Joe-Davey's Earl.
The Earl Yoders and Joe Peacheys and John Bylers of the
valley bear ancestors on their names like totems on a pole
—or else nicknames, such as Diesel Dan and Stuffy John
and Strong Sam; nicknames riddle the valley as if it were
a grammar-school playground. Earl Yoder's daughter
will be Earl A.'s Katie until she is married, when her
husband's name takes possession, front and back: John
B.'s Katie Byler.

Nearly two hundred years of narrow breeding among
the Amish and Mennonites in Big Valley have resulted
in a characteristic general appearance: thick-limbed and
low to the ground, like the deep-chested Belgian horses

on the Amish teams. In the last graduating class at the Belleville Mennonite School one of the seniors studied the genealogies of his eighteen classmates and found that every one of them was related by blood or marriage or both. The consequences of a shallow gene pool, including mental disabilities and red blood cell deficiency, are only too apparent. Some of the genes have become recognizable—the round jaw, the upturned nose, the full cheeks, and especially the strong stubby hands, with fingers as thick as carrots. The distinctive recessive gene in the valley is a blood disorder known as Pyruvate Kinase Deficient Hemolytic Anemia, which requires that the child have a complete exchange of blood at birth and that his spleen be removed about a year later.

The density of family ties can be the most impenetrable barrier to those few outsiders who try to enter the society of the valley. Several years ago the son of a wealthy corporate executive tried to join the Amish community. He attached himself to a particularly sympathetic church, drove a buggy, dressed in broadfall trousers and suspenders, learned to speak the High German dialect known as Pennsylvania Dutch, and scrupulously observed the *Regel und Ordnung* (rules and order) of the church. What finally defeated him, say people who knew him and were sorry to see him leave, was the fact that he just wasn't related. Families are usually large in the valley; sometimes, they are unusually large. A well-related individual may count a dozen brothers and sisters, as many as a hundred first cousins, not to mention in-laws or his own children and what they've produced. (When Crist K. Swarey died in May 1977, at the age of eighty-two, he left 15 living children, 135 grandchildren, and 94 great-grandchildren.) Social occasions, as a consequence, are almost always family events: reunions, marriages, burials. Even Darwin Stroup, who is from Iowa, sometimes feels cut off from the activities of his own congregation because he is not a part of "the bloodline," as he calls it, although he has been pastor of the Walnut Grove Mennonite Church for eighteen years.

In this exceedingly closed community the appearance each summer of several busloads of New York City children, most of them black or Hispanic, is a controversial and often threatening event. The Old Order Amish in the valley refuse to take the children into their homes, and even among the Beachy Amish and Mennonites the exposure of their own children to the agnosticism and sophistication of the city and the profanity of the streets is considered a risk. The fact that Darwin Stroup's daughter married one and moved to "the Queens" is a universal caution.

# Chapter 2

Only four times in his life has Darrell Jackson been up by six o'clock in the morning; the fourth time was a recent midsummer morning when he became one of nearly 12,000 children to board a bus at the New York City Port Authority or the George Washington Bridge and head for "the country"—which may be any one of the 333 rural communities from Maine to Virginia that participate in the century-old charity called the Fresh Air Fund. In Darrell's case, his destination was a Mennonite dairy farm in the Kishacoquillas Valley, which he has visited for each of the past four years, and which in fact accounts for every one of his early risings.

Darrell lives in the Van Dyke projects in the Brownsville section of Brooklyn, within wincing distance of the scream of the elevated IRT as it stops at Rockaway Avenue. From the windows of the train it is like looking down into a hot brick canyon, an eroded inferno sharply colored by the afternoon light. One can walk through the projects (they go on for blocks and blocks) and see what the architect had in mind—see, almost, the balsa-wood model, with wide spaces of painted grass, and streets lined with plastic trees. In the model, it is an acceptable place to live, humanely imagined. In the model, the trees flourish and children play in the shade; mothers stroll by pushing perambulators and old people lounge on the park benches and chat; at night, you can see the teenagers in the lavender glow of mercury lamps, holding hands and falling in love.

Part of the bitterness of existence in the Van Dyke projects is the disparity between the architect's vision and life as it is really lived in Brownsville. In reality, it is the sidewalks that are green—with shattered pop bottles—and not the naked ground. The streets that run through the projects are as pocked and rough as dried-up riverbeds. Instead of trees they are lined with unoccupied teenaged boys, shirtless and muscular, staring at passersby with idle-eyed hostility. Angry graffiti float overhead on the walls behind them, like bubbles of dialogue in a garish cartoon. Old people and women do not stroll in this neighborhood; they keep to the main routes, to the store and directly home. On the corners, where liquor is sold, the men of Brownsville slump against the walls in siesta position, their feet splayed out on the glassy sidewalks and their heads lolling to one side, like marionettes with their strings cut. Children stay close to the buildings they live in so that their mothers can watch them from the windows above, and holler five, ten, fifteen stories down to be careful, to come to dinner, not to cross the street. Inside, the elevators are jerky and eccentric. Sometimes they refuse to work at all and then you have to walk all the way up in the stairwell, which is stained with profanity and smells of urine.

Even so, many residents of the Van Dyke projects will insist that there are worse places to live. Certainly it is better to live in the projects than in the exploded slums that surround them. Jack Kott, the Fresh Air Fund's representative in the Ocean Hill–Brownsville area, calls it "probably the lowest socio-economic area in the country in terms of the lack of private property, the density of population, the number of broken families, and the number of burned-out buildings." The problems of Brownsville are typical of some other neighborhoods in Brooklyn, notably Bedford-Stuyvesant, East New York, and Bushwick—among the most degraded communities in the United States.

Brooklyn wasn't always the rubbled urban landscape it is today. Darrell's grandmother, Frannie Stone, lived until 1927 on her parents' farm in Canarsie, only a few miles south of her present home in the Brownsville projects. As a child she rode horseback to the church that stood on Avenue J and Rockaway Parkway; often she would ride through the fields to Jamaica Bay and watch the fishermen in the marshes. Frannie likes to hear her grandson describe his visits to Pennsylvania—it gives her a chance to surprise him with her knowledge of farm life, even to the best way of plucking a chicken, which she learned from her mother. From what Darrell tells her, Frannie imagines that being an Amish or Mennonite farmer in the Kishacoquillas Valley today must be very much like what it was to have been a black farmer in Brooklyn fifty years ago.

Darrell listens with half an ear; he's not interested in his roots. At ten years of age, Darrell keeps his interests to himself. His mother has to spy discreetly in his room to keep up with the latest. Usually the library books give it away—books on snakes, or allergies, or dinosaurs, or automobile repair. Sometimes she wonders if her son is going to be a scientist. He is always getting things in the mail: catalogues, and little packages from Grand Rapids or San Francisco which he snatches from the mailbox and opens privately in his room. Mrs. Jackson found the last mysterious shipment in the back of Darrell's underwear drawer, a pair of plastic glasses with concentric circles in the lenses. Mrs. Jackson supposed it was a scientific implement of some sort until she read the instructions. "X-ray glasses," they said: "See what you always *wanted* to see!" A sketch showed a man with an excited expression wearing the glasses, watching a buxom blonde pass by. Mrs. Jackson once discovered another of Darrell's purchases when she sat down to dinner: a whoopie cushion, which made a flatulent noise like a Bronx cheer when she sat on it.

Darrell does most of his shopping in the back of comic books. To his brother's annoyance he keeps his comics off limits, wrapped in cellophane and locked in a suitcase. With the exception of his single-speed Schwinn bicycle, which is parked directly beside his bed, this collection represents Darrell's biggest property investment, a total value of perhaps twenty dollars. Darrell doesn't hoard baseball cards like most of his friends, or the cards that promote popular movies and television shows, such as *Star Wars* and *Charlie's Angels*. That's all junk, he thinks, a waste of money. Comics are different because they are art, the art of fantasy and wishful thinking, and an affordable escape from the projects. His favorite character is Richie Rich, a white child on the Little Lord Fauntleroy model who is able to buy his way out of preposterous situations with his unlimited funds. Darrell reads these comics ("Every page *Rich* with humor") with only the dimmest sense of irony, or injustice. Since the middle class is virtually absent in Brooklyn's Brownsville, great wealth and great poverty seem simply like opposite sides of a coin—a perspective that is encouraged in Darrell's mind by the conspicuous success of ballplayers, dope pushers, and especially the showboating pimps, who cruise by in chinchilla coats and Cadillacs, beckoning the ghetto child's imagination to a life of Richie Rich indulgence. Darrell subscribes only partially to this fantasy. He still tells people who ask the tormenting question that he hopes to be a pro football player when he grows up (half the ten-year-old boys in Brownsville would give the same response), but lately he's been adding in a tentative voice, "—or an artist."

Darrell finances his comic book collection by selling the New York *Daily News* on Sunday mornings. He buys ten copies at the newsstand for $3.50 and sells them each for fifty cents. He has a roll of regular customers, mainly old people for whom it is worth an extra fifteen cents to avoid the trip outside. By noon Darrell is $1.50 ahead, but usually the money doesn't last until sundown. He likes to spend Sunday afternoons at the Utica Avenue Roller Rink or at the drugstore, where he can peruse the latest comics and spend the entire morning's earnings on candy and Cokes, finishing off spare pennies in the gumball machine.

There is a tough-guy swagger about Darrell that impresses his peers and usually makes the older boys smile. The truth is that he is terrified of violent confrontations and is only marginally more sophisticated about ghetto types—pimps, hookers, junkies, etc.—than a suburban child who has seen such people only on television. Darrell has never tried drugs and knows almost nothing about them. He never uses profanity at home, and when he does elsewhere he has only a vague idea of what it means. From television models of children in his situation, he knows that he is expected to be much more street smart than he actually is. He also knows that he should have strong feelings about the wretchedness of his life, but instead he is fond of his neighborhood and his friends, is more or less happy, and is full of ambivalence because of it.

He is confused about sex, and flustered by his confusion. He knows that girls are to be treated with apparent indifference, and that the more you like them the more you pretend you couldn't care less. He is uncertain about his mother's relationship to men, especially to a man named Mr. Jones, an older man who hides a bald spot with a straw fedora and often runs errands for Mrs. Jackson. Like most black families in their building, the Jacksons live on welfare and the father is "absent," as the sociologists say. In this case, the father is dead. Darrell's mother has never explained exactly how he died. Once she mentioned something about his dying "in a fire," and later she said "under fire," so that Darrell has never been sure whether his father burned to death or died in a war.

Darrell is tall for ten, with the angularity of a teenager, and a teenager's interest in fashionable clothes. He likes to dress sharp, although his wardrobe is limited by his allegiance to the Halloween combination of black and orange—the colors of the Pee Wee Pioneers football team, for which he plays wide receiver. This year when he packed to go to Pennsylvania, Darrell included a pair of gabardine slacks for church, cut-off jeans, tank tops, a few prized comic books, several changes of black or orange nylon underwear, and a book entitled *The Art in Cartooning,* which he stole from the Brooklyn Public Library. When he finished dressing for the trip—green jogging shoes, orange gabs with pleats up the legs, and a black nylon tee shirt—he planted a red number 2 pencil behind his ear to signify his art.

When a Pennsylvania preacher named Willard Parsons established the Fresh Air Fund in 1877, his aim was to rescue consumptive and crippled children from the miasmas of the city, fill them with nourishing food and clean country air, exercise them in the mountains and woods, and return them to Brooklyn in healthier condition. The first trip brought nine children to Parsons's parish in Sherman, Pennsylvania, in the Poconos. The next summer he placed more than a thousand in nearby communities. In the hundred-odd years of its operation the Fund has expanded to twelve states, draws from all five boroughs of the city, and has provided over a million free vacations to New York City children.

Although the Fund still operates a special camp for the handicapped, the children who crowded into the Port Authority with Darrell Jackson were merely poor, not ill (in fact, they needed a doctor's certificate to prove it). They were also black and Hispanic in the majority. Their hosts, almost without exception, would be white—a fact that prompts some people to believe that the Fresh Air experience is a cruel delusion for the children of the barrio and the ghetto who, because of their race or class, may never achieve the "good life" they presumably enjoy during their two weeks' vacation. Admittedly, most of these children spend five to ten hours a day in front of a television set, and so are already complexly deluded about the good life. And yet for some of them the trip acquires an importance that can frighten their parents, their hosts, and of course the children themselves, whose heightened sense of deprivation may leave them despondent for months, wised up at last.

Five slow lines shuffled toward the registrars. Behind the desks at the end of the line was a holding area surrounded by yellow barricades, where parents surrendered their children with guilty shrugs, as if they were turning them over to the authorities. Many of the younger children had never left their mothers' sides; they towed their suitcases into the holding area and stood forlorn and pale, beyond the reach of the cheerlessly waving adults.

Macy Mizell sat by herself on her suitcase reading from a year's collection of letters from Anna Louise and Rose Byler, the Beachy Amish girls whom Macy visits each summer. She was dressed in a designer tee shirt, "rainbow" jeans with multicolored stripes around the pockets, and transparent-plastic sandals called jellies. Macy is a large girl with large gestures, and a broken front tooth which her self-conscious smile cannot disguise. "It's really different in the valley," Macy says; "you can walk around barefoot and not be tippy-toeing around, watching for glass." She mimicked herself walking barefoot along Flatbush Avenue, a thought she found hilarious. When she stood to perform, the stack of letters slipped into the milling feet of the crowd. *"Don't step on that!"* she screeched, immobilizing every child within ten feet of the blast of her voice.

Macy gathered a dozen envelopes with Belleville, Pa. postmarks. "At first, I did think they were *strange,"* she says, speaking of her Belleville family. "I mean, the kids are a lot different from the kids I know. For one thing, they got a lot of animals."

She held up one of the letters, which was written in an upright and awkwardly cursive hand and torn out of a spiral notebook. "Dear Macy," she read, "we just about have a Old MacDonald farm because we have one cow named Peg, three pigs, sixteen banties, only the big ones have names. They are Mopsy, Topsy, and Doodle. There are thirteen chickens, four turkeys, three ducks named Waddle, Doddle, and Toddle, four cats named Mustard, Midnight, Ginger, and Cinammon, and one dog, Taffy." Macy shook the envelope and two wallet-sized color prints tumbled out, school pictures showing Amish girls with braided blond hair tucked under lacy white coverings. Anna Louise, the older and blonder sister, had a scolding, grown-up look and a complexion like a fruit blossom. Rose, the letter writer, had freckles and horn-rimmed glasses, and her mouth was set in a determined line, like a batter at the plate: a tomboy, for certain. "Here, listen to this," Macy continued: "P.S. I can't wait till you come. Macy, you better be at the Mount Zion Church when the bus comes, and I mean it too! Love, Rose. P.S.S. Don't you miss the bus either!"

In fact Macy had fretted all night that she might miss the bus, or worse. "I dreamt that I was on the bus coming and I was the only one, so I went to another bus and after that I kept changing buses over and over. When I got there Anna Louise and Rose weren't there so I had to wait an *hour,* and the next day was like the same day I was going home. So really I only stayed one day. I told my mother I went through suffering, for no reason. Then everything blurred. That was the end."

Macy's mother, Jolene Thomas, has been sending her daughter away through the Fresh Air Fund for five summers, since Macy was six, always to the same family in Pennsylvania. At first, it seemed like a good idea, to get her out of the house in summer, off the hot streets. "That's two weeks out of a chile's life they always be talkin' about," says Ms. Thomas. "Many kids right here ain't never been outta New York, not even to Jersey." Lately, though, she has begun to worry about Macy's "obsession." "You oughtta see her when she come back from that place. She be cryin' for a solid mont', till she go back to school. I have to, you know, beat her and tell her she got to wait till nex' year. She come back and she be talkin' jus' like them. I can't understand one word she say."

In the past year Macy has begun to think about moving to the Kishacoquillas Valley when she grows up. Although Jolene Thomas hasn't said anything, Macy has already told her that there aren't any other black people living there. "Who you gonna marry?" she once joked. "They got boys there too, Momma," said Macy. Jolene bit her lip.

Julio Ruiz, seven years old, from the South Bronx, leaned over the yellow railing and suffered the embrace of his mother, a thin, sallow woman with sunglasses and a huge floral scarf covering her head and much of her face. She tugged playfully at his curly hair, but he drew back, with his cheeks drawn and his eyes defiantly tearless. Alicia Ruiz recognized the flat, hurt look her son was giving her. She consoled him by telling him how much he was going to love the country, the clean air, the fine country smells. She loved it herself when she worked in the onion fields on Long Island. She remembers sleeping with the doors open at night and listening to the concert of katydids.

Like many children, Julio is nicely dressed in new clothes his mother has bought for the occasion. Often the hosts complain that the New York children are better dressed than their own, which suggests that the children are not so deprived as advertised. In fact the New York mother has only tried to minimize the differences her child will have to face as a city kid in the country, usually a black child in a white family, and in some instances a poor child in a rich home. Alicia Ruiz has gone so far as to have her son circumcised just prior to the trip, something she'd neglected when Julio was born, and he frequently digs his hands into his pants to scratch the irritation. Mrs. Ruiz has been attending to many unfinished duties since she learned, at age twenty-nine, that she might not live to be thirty. Her face bears the purple bruise of lupus, in an advanced state, which has made her feeble and turned her bones so brittle that sometimes when she attempts housework or washing the dishes her fingers snap and break. She has prescribed the Fresh Air vacation for Julio so that he can get out of a sick woman's house, and perhaps get used to being without her. Her frailty was apparent as she tried to pull Julio to her for another kiss. He pushed away and joined the other children.

Darrell Jackson has his mother's long face and round eyes, and when he's nervous, as he was when he said goodbye and joined the other children inside the barricades, he has a habit of rolling his eyes and flicking his pencil in an unconscious parody of Groucho Marx. He examined the round tag the diameter of a softball which had been looped around his neck at the registration desk. It gave his name and the name of the host family with whom he lives in Big Valley: the Norman Kanagys, who coincidentally have a son also ten, also named Darrell. "To me, they just like a second family," Darrell Jackson says. "They got a red barn, red brick house, about fifty-something cows, a truck outside, and upstairs in the barn it's full of hay. Downstairs they got a basketball goal with nice slippery floors and shavings all around. It's a good place to play tag 'cause you be climbin' around everywhere."

Among the children who have made the trip before there is an expectant air as they search for past acquaintances. Darrell spots Franklin Williams behind a pair of silver-rimmed shades with the initials FW in the corners. He is grooming himself with an orange Afro pick. "Dar-

*rell!"* Franklin greets him. "Whatcha say?" Darrell and Franklin are good friends in the valley. Each made his first trip four years ago, and in the country they are "next door" neighbors, although the distance from door to door is nearly three-quarters of a mile, which in the city is almost half the distance between Darrell's eighth-floor niche in the Brownsville projects and Franklin's apartment above a car service in Bedford-Stuyvesant.

"This is a terrible group of kids," Darrell observed. *"Terrible!"*

"The last bus was better," Franklin agreed. "Some of these kids are acting kinda silly." He gestured toward Ann and Aquilla Peachey, his Kishacoquillas "Mom and Dad," as he calls them, who were acting as escorts for the trip. Ann is a broad-shouldered, athletic-looking woman, who was wearing a Ban-Lon shell, a full skirt to her knees, and her long brown hair in a ponytail. Her husband Quill is a heavy, amiable man, the size of a bear, with his hair cut cleanly around his ears and slapped down with Brylcreem. They looked not so much out of place (*nobody* looks out of place in the Port Authority) as out of time—a pair of wholesome anachronisms from the Eisenhower fifties. At the moment they were standing in the center of the holding area sorting out registration problems and breaking up fights.

"Mom and Dad, they're so patient," Franklin sighed. "They love kids. I don't know how they stand them. If it was me, I'd punch 'em out."

"Yeah."

"Some of the little kids I like," Franklin conceded. *"Donny*—you met Donny?" Franklin signaled to Donny Perez, a tiny Latin with a look of intelligent apathy. Donny was roaming through the holding area eavesdropping on the conversations of other children. "You gotta meet this kid," said Franklin. "He's only eight years old, but he's a well-behaved child."

Darrell greeted the diminutive Donny. "What family you go to?" Darrell asked.

Donny shrugged. "I don't know, 'cause I never been before. What family you go to?"

"Kanagys."

"You like it? What're they like?"

"They're real churchy," said Darrell, "but they ain't Dutch."

"What's Dutch?"

"They're like white people, but they don't believe in 'lectricity. They got big beards and hats—"

"Jewish!" Donny guessed.

"Not Jewish! *Armish!*"

The escorts began segregating the children by their registration tags, which indicated whether they were going to Vermont, Connecticut, upstate New York, or Pennsylvania. Some of the children got separated from their cousins, or new friends, and they began to cry again or morosely eat their lunches. It was almost ten in the morning; the trip was already an hour late.

Ann Peachey noticed a boy in the area without the conspicuous tag. Ann asked where it was.

"I ain't got one."

"Well, where are you going? I'll see if it's at the desk."

"I ain't decided."

He ain't *decided!* Ann smiled at the thought that he imagined he could pick and choose. He wasn't even supposed to be in the holding area without his tag. "You mean you're not registered?"

"I been registered," he said, "but the people I be goin' to died."

"Died!" Ann's voice cracked in surprise.

"That's what they tole me," the boy said in a disgusted tone. Instead of a suitcase he held a brightly striped laundry bag, which he swung idly around his lanky legs. His head was large, bulbing in the rear and tapering into a pointed, prognathous jaw. His hair was shaved into a curly stubble and he had large, heavy-lidded eyes, with a scrim of suspicion across them like a nictitating membrane. And yet when he smiled—as he suddenly did—his face was engaging. "Where you goin'?" he asked.

"Pennsylvania. Big Valley."

"What's it like?"

"Oh, it's pretty! Mountains and farms, lots of animals . . ." Ann shut up; now this boy had her selling the trip to him, as if she were a travel agent. In fact, she did need extra children to replace the ones who had decided at the last minute not to go, or had overslept—station failures, they are called.

The boy bought the part about the animals. "I guess I'll go with you."

Ann called the Fund office to straighten out his registration. She found that the boy, whose name is Tyrone Howard, had, in fact, been registered to go on a previous trip but his visit had been canceled. "What happened?" she asked the representative.

"Death in the family," said the man in the office.

"Really?"

"Didn't I tole you?" Tyrone snorted. "I bet they got kilt."

The driver finally signaled that he was ready. The children struggled to lift their bags and pressed toward the gate. Ann Peachey stood in the door of the bus administering pink motion-sickness pills, orange juice, and vomit bags, while Quill gathered suitcases by the half-dozen and loaded them into the luggage compartment. Forty children filled the unlit bus. The youngest ones, five and six years old, their eyes wide and white with apprehension, twisted in their seats and watched Ann walk the aisle, counting heads. Franklin and Darrell sat in the rear, where they could monitor the traffic into the toilet, and keep their distance from the little kids up front.

The driver boarded in his gray uniform and muttered inaudibly as he surveyed his cargo. Just as he was closing the door a frantic mother banged on the side of the bus. He let her in and she delivered a cheeseburger to her son. "Sorry," she said on her way out.

"That's okay, lady," the driver said dryly to himself. She was already gone and he was pulling away.

The children were subdued as the bus maneuvered through midtown traffic toward the Lincoln Tunnel. The sun filtered through the green windows and filled the aisle with an aquatic light. A shrill voice like a chalk squeak spoke into the driver's shoulder. "Today is my birthday," said Donny Perez.

The driver yawned. He squeezed into a new lane and entered the tunnel. Simultaneously, forty hands reached for the reading lamps.

"I got seven dollars," Donny informed him. "I'm saving my money so I can buy a watch so I can tell time. I got a job."

The driver glanced abstractedly into his rearview mirror to examine the talker. He didn't find him there. He wheeled half around and discovered Donny perched on the edge of his seat, his straight black hair highlighted by the reading lamp, staring at the driver through bright black eyes with the self-possessed gaze of an undazzled

New Yorker. "Yeah, what kind a work you do, kid?"

"Wash car windows at the Shell station on Atlantic Avenue."

The driver laughed. "How you gonna wash windshields when you can't reach over the hood?"

"I miss some spots," Donny admitted, losing interest fast after the wisecrack about his height. He looked out the window at the walls of the tunnel, which had already begun to reflect light from the New Jersey orifice. "So," said Donny, trying again, "how long you been driving the Great Dane?"

*"Greyhound,"* said the driver, making a noise like a sneeze.

"Oh. Are we in Pennsylvania yet?"

Across the aisle Macy Mizell examined the records in Gwendolyn Butler's bag: a Melba Moore album, a Ralph MacDonald 45 ("Jam on the Groove"), and an album entitled "Trans-Europe Express."

"Oooh, I got that one. *La*-dahdee-la *dah!"* Macy crooned. Gwendolyn was sunk in an article about Farrah Fawcett-Majors in the *National Enquirer.* "The only thing that makes Farrah beautiful is her hair," Macy observed. Macy had wrestled her own hair into four beaded barrettes. When it is unpinned her hair stands straight up, as if she'd just plugged her toe into an electric socket.

"My boyfriend got good hair," Gwendolyn said. "I like playing with his hair. It's soft in back. That's the kind you can't braid, it's too soft."

"No nigger naps?" Macy inquired.

"Are you kidding?"

Natasha Brown, in the seat behind Macy, was dressed in tangerine "jump-suit gauchos" with clear vinyl pockets. Although she was only eight years old, her ears were pierced like Gwendolyn's and Macy's with small gold rings, and she wore plastic jellies on her feet. Her hair was glamorously oiled and braided. When the older girls started talking about hair she leaned over the seat and literally stuck her head into the conversation. "My brother's name is Reggie," she told them, "but his real name is Regiland."

"That's a *nice* name," said Gwendolyn, with sarcastic politeness. She pointedly turned away and continued her conversation with Macy. "What's your boyfriend's name?"

"Ray," said Macy.

"He cute?"

"Yeah. He got a big Afro."

"How I'm supposed to know? You got a picture?"

Natasha's head encroached farther, almost into the purse where Macy was fishing for her boyfriend's photo. "Her mamma know she kiss boys," Macy joked to Gwendolyn, and Natasha smiled coyly and rocked on her elbows on top of the seat.

"Maybe I do, and maybe I don't."

"That ain't nuthin'," Gwendolyn snorted. "You tongue him?"

Macy whooped. "She go like this," said Macy, wagging her tongue. Natasha jerked back, scandalized, and Macy laughed again, rubbing tears from her eyes.

"Well, do you tongue yours?" Gwendolyn asked her, examining Ray's picture.

Macy snatched it back. "Don't axe me my business."

Gwendolyn smiled pleasantly.

Natasha crumpled back into her seat, her brows knit in a petulant scowl. In the space next to her was a slim boy with a large round button saying RE-ELECT COUNCILMAN STEINGUT. Natasha looked at him coldly. "I hate boys," she said. "But I don't hate my father and I don't hate God."

"You forgot Jesus," said the boy with the campaign button. "Jesus is a boy."

"Jesus is a full-grown man," Natasha advised him furiously. "He died so we could live. And what's that man' name, he ate the apple and we all got in trouble?"

The boy twisted his mouth and tried to think of the man who ate the apple. "I dreamed my father died," he said instead. "He got shot. Then he was in the hospital and got out. I think he went to my gran'mamma house. Your father livin' wit' choo?"

Natasha shook her head no.

"Me neither. My father live in Georgia. Where your father live?"

"He ain't tell me where he live," said Natasha.

The bus sped through gray New Jersey.

Potato chips and bread crusts dribbled onto the floor, and empty pop bottles rolled about whenever the bus turned. The trading card of Nino Espinosa, a pitcher for the New York Mets, lay facedown in a puddle of Mountain Dew.

Ann and Quill patrolled the aisle, helping children to the bathroom and snatching the mischievous out of the luggage racks. Quill caught the emergency exit door just as it cracked open. He gave a stern reprimand to the boy who had spent five minutes working it loose. "Uh-oh," the boy explained.

Tyrone Howard, his stomach empty and his lunch uneaten, examined the head of the boy in front of him, which was suddenly an irritating presence. He leaned over the seat and whispered into the boy's ear: "You muvver have babies every week." Tyrone was nine, but he was already the tallest boy on the bus. His shaved head and sinister eyes gave him a bullying authority.

"You muvver get drunk and make fudge all over the place," the boy, whose name was Ricky, responded. Ricky may have been scared, but he knew how to play Dozens.

"You muvver is the whole front line of the Pittsburgh Steelers," Tyrone spat into the boy's other ear.

Ricky stood up. "You muvver sell *food tickets*," he said, "and she look like Jerry Lewis."

"You muvver sell *drugs!* And *you* look like Jerry Lewis!"

Ricky sensed weakness in Tyrone's response. "You muvver ain't got no hair," he suggested, noting Tyrone's scalped pate. "If you got a muvver."

"I got a muvver, Jack!" Tyrone's voice turned hysterical and his lip began to quiver. "At least I ain't got a big ubly black one like you."

"She black all right. She a charcoal-stick nigger."

"You muvver beat you every night!" Tyrone screamed. "She make drink out of pee to make ice tea! She on the commode awready."

"You ass!"

"You fuck!"

Tyrone swung his striped laundry sack, hitting Ricky squarely in the chest. Ricky reached over the seat and slapped Tyrone's ear. Quill Peachey came running, dodging children who were clogging the aisle and clucking over the profanity. "You face like a puppy turd!" Tyrone hollered as Quill wrapped him in his big arms.

"See that fist?" said Ricky, pressing his advantage. "That you muvver' tit."

Tyrone's big eyes budded with tears. He struggled in Quill's bear hug, scraping his face on Quill's rough chin.

"What you holdin' me for?" Tyrone demanded. "He be botherin' *me!*"

Quill sat down, pulling Tyrone into his lap and rocking him quietly. "I'll tell you what," Quill proposed in a soothing baritone. "Next time he bothers you I want you to turn around and say 'God bless you.' "

Tyrone tried to laugh, but it turned into a sobbing cough.

> *"Hey! bus driver,*
> *Speed up a little bit,*
> *Speed up a little bit!*
> *Hey! bus driver,*
> *Speed up a little bit,*
> *Speed up a little bit!"*

Macy and Gwendolyn were singing, although the bus driver was already going very fast. His jaw was set and even the gentle curves of the Interstate swung past so sharply that the children in the aisle hung on to the seats, as if they were standing in the face of a gale.

"This girl, her name was Sharon, we was jumpin' rope," said Macy. "She real, real fat. When she jump everybody say 'Earthquake!' "

Gwendolyn laughed. "We do that to Fat Albert, in exercise class. All the girls be on the fence and the boys on the floor. So Albert come up to the obstacles course. He be tryin' to get through the tunnel. It was that funny, right? He was goin' 'Uh-uh-uh' like he couldn't use the baffroom!"

"Couldn't use the baffroom!" Natasha echoed from her seat.

Macy peeked through the space between the seats. "Hey, girl," she addressed Natasha, "what family you go to?"

"I go with Dorcas Swarey."

"She Dutch?"

"Uh-huh."

"I thought so. You in the same church with me, right? You know Daniel and Ruth Byler?"

"Last year I seen you with 'em," said Natasha. "Ain't no clappin' in Dorcas's church."

"You can't talk bad in their house!" Macy reflected.

"'Cause they better. They not be cursin' like they do in New York, and all that."

"I really have to watch my mouth!" Macy agreed. "Like when I'm happy, I say, 'Oh, God!' And when I'm mad I say, *'Mother!'* "

Natasha nodded vigorously. "When *I'm* mad, I say, *'Father!'* "

Macy and Gwendolyn looked at each other and rolled their eyes. "Moving along!" laughed Gwendolyn, accidentally upsetting an Orange Crush in Macy's lap.

"Isn't that what's-her-name?" whispered Franklin, as Macy brushed past into the toilet.

"Macy," said Darrell Jackson.

"Didn't you like her last year?"

"She's okay." Darrell shrugged indifferently. In fact, he had been observing her in smoky glances ever since he noticed her in the holding area wearing her designer tee shirt (she was starting breasts this year). Macy had avoided Darrell's stare when she saw him looking, and her demure evasion mesmerized him and made him pine. When she walked down the aisle to the restroom, and inevitably passed Darrell, his face burned. He fiddled with his pencil and peeked at the toilet lock, which said OCCUPIED.

"You bring your baseball glove?" Darrell asked Franklin.

"You serious? I brought my glove, I brought my Yankees hat, I brought my trading cards . . ."

"How many cards you got now?"

"Five hundred and thirty-two."

"You got Mickey Rivers?"

"No."

"Too bad."

When Macy emerged, Darrell looked away, at the
turgid water of the Delaware River, as the bus bounced
into Pennsylvania.

Eddie Cato sat by himself on the edge of his seat nib-
bling the perimeter of his sandwich into a ham-and-
cheese circle. He is Puerto Rican, six years old, slight and
stunted (he weighs only 38½ pounds), with a wedge-
shaped face and nervous brown eyes. He gripped the
sandwich with both hands and looked about in quick,
jerky glances like a squirrel working on a walnut. Natasha Brown passed by, and Eddie's hand darted out and
grabbed at the coloring book she carried. Natasha kicked
him in the knee and walked blithely back to her seat. "I
kick!" Eddie hollered after her, "I kick-kick-kick you
butt!" He held his knee and sobbed, and his eyes wid-
ened with hysteria.

The children who made the trip last year remember
Eddie; especially they remember when it took three men
to carry him onto the bus back to New York. "You
shoulda heard him," Franklin recalls, "he was screamin'
so, like they was killin' him!" Now Eddie went rigid and
fell on his back into the aisle. His bawling turned keen
and loud like a siren, alarming the other children into
silence. Quill Peachey tried to pick him up but the child
thrashed so furiously that Quill feared he would hurt
himself against the metal curbs along the aisle. He patted
Eddie softly.

Eddie was one of the most troubled Fresh Air children Quill had met. It was unnerving how his behavior lurched around like unsecured cargo on the deck of a reeling ship. Most of the time he was withdrawn and silent, and even when he spoke it was in such a low voice that an adult had to stoop to hear, causing Eddie to turn shyly away and drop the rest of the sentence over his shoulder. Other times he would turn urgent, sputtering a desperate message that refused to make itself sensible, and a "fit" would overtake him. In this condition it was best to let him struggle until the paroxysm spent itself. The confidential report from the Fresh Air Fund advised that he not be placed in a home with young children, for even in apparently calm spells he could be violent. Ann Peachey had put him with Ivan and Aire Stoltzfus, a farming couple whose own children were grown. They had the reputation of being strict parents even among the sternest of the valley's believers. The message in Proverbs 13:24, "He that spareth his rod hateth his son: but he that loveth him chasteneth him betimes," is strongly held in the Amish-Mennonite tradition. Ann's opinion was that a child as volatile and disturbed as Eddie required a firm hand, one that could punish as lovingly as it embraced.

Eddie screamed until his voice turned raw and the sound itself was painful to hear, but by then the other children had grown bored and angry. The traffic in the aisle resumed, squirming past Quill and stepping over Eddie's flailing legs. After a while the rhythm of Quill's steady pat began to insinuate itself, and the demon inside Eddie Cato tired. His body went visibly limp. Quill picked him up and laid him in his seat.

"How many more minutes?" Natasha asked Ann Peachey in Allentown, 150 miles east of Big Valley. The bus was idle on the side of the road in front of a Burger King, into which the driver had disappeared. The air conditioner was off and the bus was beginning to bake. Cars whooshed by on the side of the highway, making a noise like breaking waves. After twenty minutes the driver returned, chewing ice from a paper cup. Just before he boarded he tossed the cup over his shoulder, stuck a toothpick into his mouth, then climbed back to the controls.

Tyrone was trying to remember the words to the song his brother had taught him. "*Rudolph the red-nosed—* No, wait." He started again.

> "*Rudolph the red-nosed cowboy*
> *Had a little shiny gun!*
> *When if you ever saw him*
> *You woulda sure and run!*
> *When—when Santa came to . . .*
> Oh.
> *When the sheriff came to . . .*
> Wait a minute.
> *Rudolph the red-nosed cowboy*
> *Had a little shiny gun!*
> *When if you ever saw him*
> *You woulda sure and run!*
> *Then one froggy Christmas eve*
> *Santa said to me,*
> *'Rudolph with your gun so bright*
> *Come and shoot my wife tonight.'*
> *When if you ever—*

I mean, uh . . . I forgot the rest."

A Pennsylvania state trooper was lurking over a hill just beyond the Reading exit. The Greyhound passed doing better than 80. A moment later the bus was back on the side of the road, and the driver was sitting in the squad car. The children crowded to the front to watch. Some of them speculated that the driver would go to jail, and abandon them on the Interstate. That thought went through Quill's mind as well.

Suddenly the driver jumped out of the car and strode angrily back to the bus. The children disbanded and were sitting innocently in their seats when the glowering driver came on. "I don't wanna hear another peep outta you kids," he warned, shoving the ticket into the shirt pocket of his uniform.

"I ain't thinkin' 'bout that boy," Macy told Gwendolyn. "I ain't get along with Virgo. My sister is a Virgo. You know what boy I'm talkin' 'bout? Darrell?"

"Which one?"

"Not on this row. Over there by the window with the pencil behind his ear."

"That's him," said Natasha. "He cute."

"Oooh, she *pointed* at him!" Macy sank in her seat and hid. "Now he gonna know we be talkin' 'bout him."

*"That crazy broad!"* Darrell shivered. "She got me all mix up! Now, what was you sayin'?"

"I wasn't even talkin' to you," said Franklin. "Me and Donny was talkin'."

Darrell looked at him hopelessly.

"That's right, he was talking to me," Donny agreed.

"It's real quiet in Big Valley," said Franklin, returning to his previous conversation. "It's a different world. I used to have trouble sleepin', like at night? 'Specially the first year. You know, without any traffic to put you to sleep. It be country noises at night goin' down."

"I just threw up in the bathroom," Julio Ruiz confessed to Tyrone. Julio had been asleep for most of the trip (unconsciously scratching at his circumcision, which made some of the girls laugh). He woke up nauseated and rushed to the bathroom, returning pale and unsteady.

Tyrone sneered. "I never get sick," he assured Julio. " 'Cept on airplanes, sometime. When they go real far and serve breakfast."

At Harrisburg, the bus ran beside the wide, white-rocked Susquehanna, which parallels a protracted strip of franchise food stores and budget motels. Natasha viewed the rushing water and wondered if there were sharks. Macy looked out the other window and wished she could stop for French fries and a Coke. When the bus had crossed the bridge it began to climb into the ridge country along the Juniata River. A four-lane highway ran on top of a long, twisting ridge, bare of trees on the summit. The highway's median strip was covered with wild flowers.

The bus eventually dropped off the ridge and soon exited into the Kishacoquillas Valley. At the northern end, where the bus entered, the mountains on either side open four miles wide. It was like entering the wide end of a horn—a horn of plenty, it seemed, for the fields were full of waving green corn, looking almost black in the green glass of the bus windows. On the left side of State Road 655 a billboard with a skull and crossbones warned, FOR THE WAGES OF SIN IS DEATH. The bus passed creeks and bridges, houses of old ruddy brick, long fence rows and cows napping beside white stones in shaded pastures, bearded men working in the waist-high corn behind teams of muscular blond horses, and boys in straw hats walking on the roadside, staring back.

"That's where you're going to stay, with my brother and his wife," Ann told Tyrone, pointing to the mountain on the right. "Way up in the woods."

Tyrone grinned. "I'mana play with the animals," he announced to the bus. "She say it has goats up there. Ain't they got goats?" he hollered to Ann.

"Well, they have two goats," Ann confirmed.

"What else?"

"A dog."

"What else?"

"Chickens."

"What else?"

"A cat."

"What else?"

"That's all."

Tyrone sat down, satisfied.

"When we get there I'll be talkin' with Luke," said Franklin. "We be foolin' aroun' in the parkin' lot for a while, maybe play baseball."

"Basketball," said Darrell. "Basketball in the Kanagy barn."

"Hey, yeah!"

"There's Ruth's mother's house!" Macy screamed. "Oh, God! And the church is over the hill! I can't believe it!"

# Chapter 3

Darrell and Norman Kanagy sat in the cab of their pickup truck waiting for the Greyhound to arrive. Norm slept, with his head and neck arched over the seat and his mouth partly opened, while his son read another Hardy Boys mystery, number forty-five for Darrell out of fifty-seven books in the series. Darrell slumped in the seat with his feet propped on the dash, the book balanced on his knees. His toes spilled out each side of his worn-out, outgrown tennis shoes. He has blond hair in bangs to his eyebrows, blue eyes, and his mother's aquiline nose. For nine years of his life Darrell had heard how much he takes after her side of the family, but suddenly in his tenth year he came to resemble his father, not only in the level grin and wide-set eyes they have always shared, but in physique as well—Norm's thick torso and short muscular limbs. Both wore blue jeans and sleeveless white tee shirts—their invariable summer attire, outside of church.

In the same way Darrell Jackson is a product of the Brownsville ghetto, Darrell Kanagy typifies the culture of the Kishacoquillas Valley, which is notably rural, religious, and relatively free of the influence of television. It is this last point that chafes Darrell Kanagy. He is avid for news about the television culture and often urges his parents to visit in homes that have a set. So far, Norm has withstood his son's sarcastic commentary on the primitiveness of life without television, especially life without the Philadelphia Phillies games that are broadcast on the Altoona station. Norm thinks television is an evil influence, a violent and carnal contaminator, and although he has told his son that he is opposed to television on moral grounds, his principal argument has been that it isn't worth buying a set in Big Valley anyway, because the mountains screen all the signals and even the Altoona station is so fuzzy that you can't read the numbers of the players. He proved the point once during the World Series, when he capitulated and rented a set. He enjoyed watching the games himself, although he was a little abashed at sitting idle for such long periods, as if he were sick. Recently the cable from Huntingdon, carrying a variety of clear-channel entertainments, invaded the south end of the valley. It hasn't reached Norm's farm yet, but his church, the Walnut Grove Mennonite, has already suffered the refutation of the fuzzy-picture argument, with the result that television owners have become the majority of the congregation.

"Dad, I'm gonna walk around with the other guys," said Darrell when he finished the chapter.

"Umm," Norm acknowledged from his subconscious.

Darrell stretched and wandered through the parking lot. Nearly a hundred people waited for the bus, and he knew them all, at least by name. Many of them were relatives. Darrell never feels anonymous in Big Valley.

He found one of his first cousins, Galen Peachey, leaning against a locust tree, his hands in his pockets. Galen has a reputation for being shy, a reticent talker, who likes to walk for hours in the woods with his dog. Galen was waiting for his Fresh Air companion, Stephen Washington, who is also shy. The year before they had each spent a lot of time reading.

"Hey, Galen!" Darrell shouted. "Hey, I got a new joke!"

Galen winced. He hates the way Darrell tells jokes, with his head down and his eyes on his shoes as if he were giving an oral report.

"A smart boy and a stupid boy are in a store," Darrell began, "and the smart boy is trying to show the stupid boy how to make a sale. So he says, 'Got anything for sale?' and the stupid boy says he doesn't know and the smart boy says, 'Don't say that, say *shoelaces.*' " Darrell laughed. "So the smart boy asks if he's got anything for sale, and the stupid boy says, 'Shoelaces.' 'How much are they?' The stupid boy says he doesn't know. 'Don't say that,' says the smart boy, 'say they're two for a nickel. Now how much are these shoelaces?' 'Two for a nickel.' 'Are they any good?' 'Don't ask me,' says the stupid boy. 'Don't say that,' says the smart boy, 'say some are, some aren't. Now how much are these shoelaces?' 'Two for a nickel.' 'Are they any good?' 'Some are, some aren't.' And the smart boy says, 'In that case, I don't think I'll buy any.' 'Suits me,' says the stupid boy. And the smart boy says, 'Don't say that, say if you don't, someone else will.' Then the smart boy's mother came and got him, and he told the stupid boy to tell this to the next person who asks."

Galen's polite grin ached on his face. He stared over Darrell's shoulder down State Road 655, where the bus would appear.

Darrell continued. "Pretty soon a stranger came in and says 'Hey fella, what's the name of this town?' 'Shoelaces,' says the stupid boy. The stranger asks how many people live there. 'Two for a nickel.' 'Are they all as dumb as you?' says the stranger. 'Some are, some aren't.' And the stranger says, 'How would you like me to punch you in the nose?' 'If you don't,' says the stupid boy"— Darrell began to giggle—" *'someone else will'!'*"

Galen laughed thinly. "That's pretty funny."

Fresh Air children have been coming to the Kishacoquillas Valley since 1893, when a fruit grower named Jefferson H. Peachey heard of the Fund and arranged a trip through the New York *Tribune,* which until it went out of business was the Fund's principal sponsor. Norm's grandfather, Jake Kanagy, an Amishman of the yellow-top order, recalls seeing old Jeff Peachey with some of the first Fresh Airs. It was easy to spot the old man because he always wore a distinctive stovepipe hat, and in the summer his carriage was full of children. Then, as now, they were the major interruption in the familiar, familial rhythm of the valley. Then they were white children, most of them Irish and Italian, many Catholics. Black children began to come in large numbers after the middle sixties, and became predominant when hosts were no longer permitted to select the race of their child.

In the history of the valley the only black people who ever lived between the mountains were three slaves belonging to Major John Wilson, a Presbyterian, who employed them to construct the handsome brick house now owned by Norm's Amish grandfather. The slaves are reputed to be buried in unmarked graves in a small cemetery with a white rail fence, which sits like a boxing ring on the hill above the Wilson house. After a lapse of 230 years another black man, who was working for the state highway department, lived in a house trailer at the north end of the valley. But he stayed only a few months, until construction carried him west, and no one actually thought of him as a resident. Except for the annual visits of Fresh Air children, blacks are rarely seen. Occasionally black people from Huntingdon pass through and stop for gas or, if it's Wednesday, stop for the flea market at the Belleville Sale Barn. But there are still people in the valley who have never seen a black adult.

Consequently, racial attitudes in the valley are almost entirely uninformed by experience. The Mennonites and the Amish generally understand black culture only by its "influences," and the influences they associate with blacks are violence, idleness, drunkenness, broken families, welfare, sensuality, and city living—virtually a catalogue of primary sins in the Apollonian culture of the Kishacoquillas Valley. Since the Fresh Air children are drawn from the worst slums in New York City, they are usually well acquainted with these influences and plenty of others, which they can sometimes expand upon to the open-mouthed amazement of their hosts.

Nor is the valley free of the racial fears that surround it—fears that blacks will move in and bring their urban customs with them. Slurs—such as "I hear it's getting pretty dark over Huntingdon way"—are fairly common in discussions of race, particularly with the Old Orders. The epithet "nigger" sounds odd in this pious community, but it can be heard, if the issue is pressed.

The bus could be seen from a long way off, an apparition with sun flaring on chrome and glass. Since buses of this size almost never pass through the valley, everyone who saw it knew that the Fresh Airs were back again, for better or worse, and that for the next couple of weeks they would be everywhere: at the store or in church, playing ball in the pasture, hanging around during choir practice, gorging at weenie roasts, pestering cows in the milking parlor, buying things, breaking things, stealing things, wading in the stream, hiking in the forest, getting in fights, getting bitten, getting lost, setting fires, throwing tantrums, throwing up—and generally increasing the level of havoc in the entire community, so that nobody would feel completely at ease until the bus returned and swallowed the lot of them, and with a full belly dissolved on the horizon.

But now the bus was bringing, not taking, and the parents in the parking lot watched with last-minute anxiety. Every year a few Fresh Air children are injured, getting their hands caught on a blade, or falling out of a loft, or being kicked by a nervous animal. Several have been killed, most frequently by drowning. Ann Peachey remembers the awful occasion during Franklin Williams's second summer when he was hit by a car while riding his bicycle. It opened a long gash on his head when he hit the windshield (the scar is covered by his luxuriant Afro), but nothing was broken. Franklin blames himself for letting down his guard. "It never woulda happen in Brooklyn," he told the lady who hit him. He often sees her when he comes to the valley (she still drives the same black Ford), and waves as she drives cautiously by. Although the Fund carries extensive liability insurance to protect the hosts, fear of lawsuits is never completely absent among the Amish and Mennonites, whose religious convictions forbid them to contest in court.

The bus dipped under a rise, then reappeared, close enough now that the children in the lot began to wave. The bus whined and geared down as it got trapped behind a yellow-top Amish buggy, the horse clopping quickly and sensing anxiously the huge machine behind him. Suddenly the bus roared past and left the horse shaking his head at the odor of diesel exhaust.

Anna Louise and Rose Byler circled the Greyhound

when it rolled to a stop. They tried to spot Macy among the gesturing shadows behind the bottle-green glass. Eleven-year-old Anna Louise fussed like a worried mother.

"Oh, I hope she didn't miss the bus. That'd be just like her!"

"She's here all right. I just know it," said Rose. Rose wore a long-sleeved blue dress in a heavy polyester, and the heat drew bubbles of perspiration from her freckled forehead and upper lip. Her hexagonal black glasses were held together across her nose with a strip of white adhesive tape.

"Oooh, look at the long dresses!" laughed Gwendolyn, inside the bus. "Boy, ain't they old-fashioned? And them boys with the trousers!"

Macy ignored her. She saw Anna Louise and Rose searching the filmy windows of the bus, waving at shadows. Rose was standing tiptoe, mouthing words Macy couldn't hear, but Macy lip-read her name and waved to the girls frantically. Tears streamed from her eyes. "I'm here! I'm here!" she sobbed. She began to jump up and down, waiting for the door of the bus to open. Suddenly, she broke into song. *"Come on, come on!"* she sang. *"Have a Pepsi day!"*

Ann Peachey disembarked and addressed the waiting crowd. "Some of you are going to be disappointed," she warned. "A lot of children didn't make it this year. We have a few extra children who we'll try to match up. As they come off I'll call the name of the host family."

"Oh, no!" Rose struck her forehead, then grabbed at her stomach as if she were going to throw up. Anna Louise chewed on her knuckles.

The children filed slowly off the bus, pensive and blinking as if they were just coming out of a matinee on 42nd Street. Satiny jogging shorts, brilliantly colored, and tee shirts advertising Adidas sneakers, Triumph motorcycles, and Foxy Ladies gleamed in the sunshine beneath globular Afros and hydra-headed pigtails and intricate corn-row braids and, of course, Tyrone's convict stubble. A quiet moment of mutual amazement settled in the parking lot as the New Yorkers stood in front of their bags waiting to be claimed.

"Oh, she did too come!" shouted Rose when Macy Mizell stepped off the bus, dabbing at her tears. Macy hugged the Byler girls, then greeted Ruth Byler, the mother of Anna Louise and Rose and five other children, including a new baby boy who was napping on her shoulder. Ruth was still heavy from pregnancy and she met Macy with a weary smile. While Macy examined the new baby, Rose surreptitiously studied the fabric in her designer tee shirt. Three of the younger children, all boys, rushed in circles around Macy's long legs, as if she were a maypole.

Daniel Byler, in a blue shirt and dark broadfall trousers with two suspenders, stood to one side pulling on his beard, a posture he often takes when he teases his children. "Why, I don't believe this is our Fresh Air," he said to Elmer, his oldest son. "There's been a terrible mistake, already."

"Dad! She is *so!*" Rose said, horrified.

"No, I'm sure of it. Our Fresh Air was only this high." Daniel indicated a spot level with his shoulder. "This one's bigger than me."

"She's *grown,*" Anna Louise explained in an exasperated voice, although she, too, was surprised to see Macy larger than her parents.

"There he is!" shouted Darrell Kanagy when Darrell Jackson appeared in the door of the bus.

"He's really stretched out this year," Norm observed.

"Yeah," said Darrell, "and he's wearing a pencil. Whaddaya s'pose *that* means?"

Esther Peachey, Galen's mother, is a big woman with broad shoulders and a prominent round jaw, pale glasses, and a blond beehive hairdo. She remembers what she thought, as she searched for her previous Fresh Air child among the faces coming off the bus, when she saw Tyrone Howard. "I noticed him right away. I thought, 'Gee, I wonder who'll get that boy?' And just then Ann called my name."

Esther and Galen glanced at each other. Galen looked alarmed. "What happened to Stephen Washington?" he demanded when Ann introduced him to Tyrone.

"He just didn't make it, Galen. But I'm sure you're going to get along with Tyrone."

Galen is a month older than Tyrone (both were approaching their tenth birthdays), but he stood nearly a head shorter. Tyrone sized him up from head to toe and paused momentarily at the sight of Galen's sneakers, an off-brand variety that Esther had bought at Shoe City. Tyrone smiled. He does have a nice smile. "I like your rejects, sucker," he said, still smiling.

Tyrone's shoes were orange crepe-soled sandals with extra-long laces, which wrapped around his ankles and tied above his calves, "Roman"-style.

"Tyrone, this is Janet," said Esther, presenting her fifteen-year-old daughter, a tan blond with silver braces in her mouth.

"Where did you get the name Tyrone?" Janet asked. "I never heard it before."

"You know who is Tyrone Power? My muvver name me after him."

"Who?"

"You don't see him sometime on the late movie?"

"We don't have a TV," Janet said dryly.

"It broke?"

"You have a TV in your house?" asked Galen, letting his envy show.

Tyrone turned huffy. "Sure I got TVs. I got six of 'em. One in every room and some more in the basement."

"We don't have time to watch television in the country," Esther explained in a cheery voice, tossing Tyrone's laundry sack into the rear of her Japanese station wagon.

Tyrone's jaw hung open while he considered the implications. "They ain't tole me I be goin' someplace with no TV," he said slowly. "How I'm gonna watch *Charlie's Angels*?"

"What's *Charlie's Angels*?" asked Galen. Tyrone looked at him uneasily.

"You'll find something else to do," Esther assured him.

After the other families had disappeared with their Fresh Air children, Ivan and Aire Stoltzfus stood to one side for a word with Ann Peachey. The family Stoltzfus belongs to a schismatic group known as the Holdeman Church, a fact anyone in the valley would recognize by the black babushka on Aire's head and Ivan's full beard and mustache. Ivan has a florid complexion, a pocked and swollen nose, and eyes magnified by thick lenses. Aire is a strong-looking woman with big hands and a kind face. Despite their reputation for harsh discipline, they are known in the valley as especially charitable people. Every year they contribute livestock and home-canned foods to church relief programs, and they have been taking in Fresh Air children since the first year of their marriage, thirty-two years ago.

Ann did not notice them at first, and when she did it took a moment for her to recognize what was wrong.

"We just wondered why little Eddie didn't make it this year—" Aire began.

*"Isn't he with you?"* Ann cried. "He got off the bus, I'm sure!" Ann rushed back into the bus and looked behind the seats and in the lavatory. "Oh, my! I called out his name and I guess I just assumed you had met him!"

"We never saw him."

"He's so little he could've slipped off somewheres. Oh, and his suitcase is gone!"

"He can't have gotten far then, the little fella."

Ann got the driver to search the luggage compartments and sent Franklin Williams and her son Luke to look in the church.

"Could he have gone with another family, d'ya suppose?"

"I wouldn't think so. He maybe slipped into the cornfield behind the church."

Ivan Stoltzfus investigated that possibility by squatting on his haunches and waddling from row to row, staring under the canopy of leaves down the long, unvarying columns of cornstalks for any sign of Eddie Cato's legs. In the meantime his wife took the family Ford north on State Road 655.

Half a mile later she found him, a skinny sticklike figure towing a gray Samsonite two-suiter at his heels. Aire pulled over on the shoulder ahead and let Eddie catch up to her.

"Why hello, Eddie, can I give you a ride?" She waited for him with a wry look that was also a little hurt.

Eddie looked nervously at the sky. His thick black hair was bluntly cut and fit on his head like a too-large bathing cap. In profile he has a fine straight nose and a sharp chin pointing down at the same angle. He mumbled something Aire couldn't hear.

"What's that?" She knelt down and put a hand on his shoulder.

"Goin' New York."

"Are you, then? Wouldn't you stay for supper first? I made a big blackberry cobbler for you. You remember the blackberry cobblers you ate last year? I never seen a boy who could eat cobblers like that!"

Eddie didn't respond.

"We got your room all red up. You remember our house, don't you? The big white house on the other mountain, you can see it from here. Look, Eddie, on the hillside there above the road, the big white house with the peach trees—"

*"Don't wanna go white house!"* Eddie screamed.

Aire took a slow breath. She was afraid that Eddie would throw a fit right there on the side of the road with all the horse droppings and the peelings of retreaded tires, and if he did she knew she wouldn't be able to restrain him by herself.

"Don't wanna go white house! Goin' New York."

Aire spoke again very softly. "Look at that mockingbird on the fence over there, singing his song. Remember the sound of the birds in the morning? You couldn't sleep, they made so much noise. And how you used to feed the fish in the pond above the house? I waited feeding them today so you could stand on the dock and feed them like you did last year. Remember?

Why, the water just boiled when you threw them pellets out! And this morning we had a surprise visitor. A puppy dog come down our lane and was ahanging 'round Ivan's workshop until we had to give him a bite to eat. Now we've got him, like it or not. I guess he'd like a little boy to play with, already. Ivan was going to build him a house but we just can't decide what to name the wee pup . . ."

Eddie muttered inaudibly.

"What was that?"

"David."

"That's his name, then. David. Don't you want to go see him?"

Eddie nodded, and let Aire hug him. She picked him up in a single easy motion, and as she did she noticed Ivan ambling toward them with his thumbs in his suspenders, following the trail inscribed by the Samsonite suitcase.

"You found him," he noted.

Eddie's head spun sharply when he heard the man's voice. Aire dreaded this moment, for last year Eddie was frightened of her husband and, indeed, any other man he happened to see. (Fear of men seemed to be a common problem among Fresh Air children who had no fathers in their homes.) But instead of tightening up, Eddie smiled broadly and wiggled his thumbs in Ivan's direction.

" 'Eeey, man! ¿Que pasa?"

Aire was relieved, but startled at the randomness of his mood change.

Ivan's bright red face burst into a smile like a ripe tomato cracking in the sun. "Heeey!" he laughed, wiggling his thumbs in return.

# Chapter 4

The map in the Allensville Post Office (Zip Code 17002) marks with tiny squares every house in the valley. Most of the squares front on a black line running through the middle: State Road 655, which serves as Main Street for both Allensville and Belleville. The Mount Zion Church is between these two villages, almost at the very center of the valley. Parallel to 655 on either side are Back Mountain Road and Front Mountain Road. The "back" mountain, in the valley vernacular, is Stone Mountain, the western escarpment, and the "front" is Jacks Mountain to the east. A car running north on any of these three roads is said to be headed "down the valley," toward the wide bowl full of sun of the rolling valley floor. The other direction, "up the valley," is darker, where the mountains begin to loom together to form the "tight end," where the Presbyterians live.

Along State Road 655 the view is always bustling, like a Grandma Moses painting. The landscape is neatly divided into well-tended rectangles full of purposeful activity—the pastures, fields, barnyards, pigpens, gardens—all quilted together. Because the sides of the valley rise gradually away from each other, like grandstands in a stadium, the entire length of the valley is always on view, and of course so is everyone in the valley as soon as he steps out-of-doors—visible to all for as far as the eye can see. A man can look for miles and see the moving dot that must be his brother working in the fields, or his brother's wife shaking out a rug, and they can see him in turn, cutting his alfalfa before the rain comes. One grows used to the perpetual surveillance by a thousand eyes, and from above by the eye of God.

When Quill and Ann Peachey arrived at their house at the bend on Back Mountain Road, Franklin Williams ran to the fence and looked out over the valley. The blue cornflowers and white blooms of the huckleberry vines on the roadside repeated the colors of the clouds and the sky. Just below was Norman Kanagy's farm, barely a mile from the Mount Zion Church down a dry dirt road that cuts between Norm's pastures. Franklin could see the Darrells standing in the bed of Norm's pickup, holding on to a rail on top of the cab, with their hair pressed back in the wind and a tail of dust swirling behind them. Up on 655 the car carrying Donny Perez was headed up the valley to the Alphie Kauffman farm; Julio Ruiz was going the other way, to the Fred Peacheys. In White Hall, an inconsiderable settlement between Allensville and Belleville, a black Volkswagen stopped at a little cottage across the road from the general store and the tangerine speck of Natasha Brown emerged. Dorcas Swarey, an Amishwoman in a gray dress and a black apron, was almost undiscernible beside her. On Front Mountain Road, directly across the valley from where Franklin stood, the Bylers' black Dodge turned into the drive, beside a two-story green frame house on the edge of a cornfield. Its porch was shaded by apple trees and a line of laundry flapped noisily in back.

But the sound Franklin heard was Luke Peachey impatiently slapping his baseball mitt. Luke was bored with this vista; it has confronted him almost every day of his thirteen years of life. Luke is his mother's image: he has her wide mouth (and enormous smile) and rangy, athletic carriage. He also has the nervous tic characteristic of his mother's family—the Hartzler blink—which gives the impression, when he is smiling, that he is flirting, or else grimacing in a high wind. Luke tossed the ball in the air and caught it himself. "C'mon, Franklin! Let's play!"

Franklin is also thirteen, but he is shorter and a little plump, with a big rear end and a round face. He didn't answer Luke at first; he was praying.

Franklin is a Christian. Ann Peachey recalls that the first thing he told her when he got off the bus, the third year he came, was "Mom! I'm saved!" It was the summer after Franklin's own mother died of kidney disease at the age of twenty-eight. She left behind three children. Franklin, ten at the time, was the youngest. He always reproached himself for that. "If only I'da been older," he told Ann, "I coulda give her one of my kidneys. It woulda worked, I bet."

After his mother died, Franklin's sister went to live with an aunt in a high-rise project on Atlantic Avenue, and Franklin and his older brother, Robert, moved in with their paternal grandmother, Lulu Williams, in a fourth-floor walkup in Bedford-Stuyvesant. The block he lives on stands between a renovated section and a burned-out section, and it's a contest to see which will claim it. One corner of the block has an apartment house that is being repainted in a sunny lemon color; the other corner is black from an arsonist's fire that spread two doors before it was stopped.

Although Ann and Quill Peachey come to New York almost every year to escort a Fresh Air trip, Franklin has never invited them to his home. It's part of his life that he hides from them, not just because his neighborhood is dangerous, with an edginess in the hot, treeless streets that always seems close to riot. Franklin knows that Ann and Quill have seen enough of New York to expect the charred windows, and the hoodlums stripping cars in broad daylight, and the angry gestures from men drinking out of paper bags. What he's afraid they won't understand is that in an obscure, frightened way he loves where he lives, and couldn't bear the embarrassment of their judgment.

The stairwell leading to Lulu Williams's apartment is a dump for broken appliances. Her old gas range is there, along with two refrigerators from neighbors long gone. Inside the apartment, Franklin will admit, is "nice," with clean linoleum floors, turquoise walls, and a Mexican painting of a flamenco dancer on black velvet. Lulu keeps the furniture covered in a nubby plastic so that the fabric underneath is as pristine as the day it came from the store. Like most of her neighbors, Lulu tries to stint on utilities, so that in the summer the apartment is dark and hot and in the winter it is dark and cold.

Franklin and Robert share a room with a large television set and two narrow beds. Each boy has an expensive AM/FM transistor radio, and a dressertop full of cosmetics. Franklin uses several popular colognes and an array of hair dressings, including Afro-Sheen and Dax pomade, for "short breaking hair." Actually, Franklin's hair forms a rich, fluffy Afro, very becoming with his wide face and high forehead. His skin is naturally light, so he doesn't have to use Robert's Ultra Bleach and Glow.

On the walls there are pictures of the Six Million Dollar Man and Mickey Rivers (the center fielder for the New York Yankees, and Franklin's idol), and a Polaroid photograph of Franklin looking like a commando, in a green beret and sunglasses—part of the uniform of the Abubekah Youth Patrol, a Masonic organization Franklin joined at the urging of his grandmother, who is a member of the Eastern Star, the women's auxiliary. "You go through life and you have problems, and you in that order and the order take care of you," Lulu advised him. "It's worldly wide."

Lulu makes no secret of her dislike for Franklin's mother. When he misbehaves, Lulu complains that he's "sneaky—like your mother was." When he's good, she compares him with her own son, Franklin's father, a New York City policeman who died when Franklin was five. Franklin used to think that his father died in the line of duty, but when he was older someone in the neighborhood told him his father was stabbed in a barroom brawl, in an argument over money.

All Franklin has to remember his mother by, other than his grandmother's recriminations, is the suitcase, compact, and nightgown that his mother took to the hospital, a half-dozen get-well cards that were in her room, and a pair of bongo drums she gave him before she died. Franklin keeps the suitcase with his mother's effects under his bed, and he lets nobody see it. That started a rumor in the neighborhood. "You got a suitcase wit' you muvver in it!" his best friend finally accused him. "No, she's not a witch!" said Franklin. "She buried in the ground. I don't want none of my relatives cremated. My mother, my father—they both buried in the ground."

Franklin serves as an usher at Deliverance Temple on DeKalb Avenue. He often sees Natasha Brown there. She looks up to him. Of all the children who make the trip to Big Valley each year, Franklin is the best known and generally the most respected, especially by girls. He has wonderful manners, and he takes care of how he looks; his Afro is immaculately groomed and shiny, and he dresses with elegance. In church he wears a three-piece Pierre Cardin suit, baby blue, with a dark blue shirt open at the neck, suede shoes, and the lightweight nylon socks that the kids call "churchies." Sometimes girls write him letters, and that bothers him because he doesn't like forward girls.

When Franklin graduates from high school he wants to move to Big Valley, to the "beloved community" of believers, even though it will mean giving up sharp clothes, jewelry, and the Masons. He plans to work the Sperry–New Holland plant, where Quill is a welder of heavy machinery. Quill thinks that Franklin will get the job if he applies, since he's heard that the company is under federal pressure to recruit minorities.

Franklin hopes that his grandmother will come with him to Big Valley; they could find a nice house and he would support her, and she would accept Christ in her heart. Every Sunday Franklin fills out prayer cards requesting that "my grandma and my brother come saved," but whenever he brings up the subject Lulu's attention wanders and Robert makes fun of him. His brother actually began riding a different train to school after Franklin started proselytizing sleepy-eyed commuters, and handing out cards that looked like Master Charge cards and said, across the orange and gold circles, GIVE CHRIST CHARGE OF YOUR LIFE. At home or at school Franklin always prays over his food, even if no one else does. When he prays, he closes his eyes and pinches the bridge of his nose, as if he is agonizing.

"Franklin! Let's play!"

A little Japanese station wagon came around the bend and passed in front of the Peacheys' house. Tyrone sat sullenly in the back. Franklin waved, then turned around to play ball. His eyes were wet and bright in the sun.

Tyrone did not wave back. He and Galen stared out opposite windows. Tyrone sang in a muffled voice so that only Galen could make out the words. The tune was the theme from *The Bridge on the River Kwai:*

> *"Rejects! are make your foots feel fine!*
> *Rejects! they cost a dollar forty-nine.*
> *Rejects! just say rejects!*
> *And rejects!*
> *Or rejects!*
> *Or now."*

Galen looked at his shoes and again out the window. "You're nothing but a queer," he muttered.

"Who you callin' a queer, Jack?" Tyrone demanded in an angry whisper. "You don't even know what that word is."

"I know all right, but I bet you don't."

"Somebody who tell lies."

Esther looked over her shoulder. "What are you boys talking about?"

For a second they looked caught and chastened. "Uh-oh," said Tyrone. Galen began to snicker. Tyrone covered his face with his hand and slid down in his seat. Galen pounded his leg and laughed in barking gasps. Esther and Janet looked at each other in confounded amusement.

"I've got a feeling this summer won't be so quiet as last," Esther observed.

Outside, Holsteins grazing near the road glanced up from their ruminations and gave Tyrone a dull, inebriated stare. Animals excite Tyrone, but he has bad luck with them. He rakes the neighborhood where he lives for stray puppies and injured birds, and brings them home, where they quickly die. Once he purchased a pair of garter snakes named Nipper and Queenie, a $5.70 investment, which he housed in the living room in an aquarium where goldfish had briefly lived. The snakes died within the week. Nipper lost a fight with a neighbor's cat; Queenie had the misfortune of crawling under a rocking chair just as Mrs. Howard was sitting down. Before Tyrone came on the Fresh Air trip his dog, the only animal to survive Tyrone's affections, got distemper and spent a week behind a tree cowering and coughing and refusing to eat. Mrs. Howard hoped the old mutt would wait until Tyrone was gone, but he died the day before the bus trip. Tyrone spent the afternoon trying to dig a grave in the impenetrable soil.

The Peacheys live on the side of Stone Mountain, up a rutted dirt road in a two-story mountain cabin that Kore Peachey is renovating. From their front porch Kore and Esther can see the entire valley, which unrolls in front of them in blocks of green. On the rises stand the red barns and brick houses of their neighbors, and the white silos with the Blue Star trademark. In the orchards above the fields there are orioles and indigo buntings.

Tyrone bolted from the car. "This place is *yours?*" he cried. Galen shrugged. Tyrone picked up a couple of stones from the drive and threw them at the billies watching him from a bluff above the house. "C'mere, goats!" The goats fled into the woods.

"What's that dog' name?"

"Prince." Galen held his arms as if he felt chill.

"Sic 'em, Prince! Git them goats!"

Prince, a black sheepdog of mixed heritage, backed under the station wagon.

"Bike!" Tyrone hollered. He ran to Galen's Schwinn and rode it once around the drive, then pointed it down the slope of the Peacheys' precipitous front yard. He traveled about a hundred feet before smashing into a stone fence and flying head first into a tree.

Galen raced down the hill to examine the wreckage of his bicycle. "Why didn't you put on brakes, already?"

"Brakes?" said Tyrone, collecting himself from the broken spokes. "Your bike got brakes, too?"

Galen clenched his teeth and carried his bicycle up the hill. *"Queer, queer, queer!"* he cursed to himself.

Darrell Kanagy lay mute across his bed reading a comic book while Darrell Jackson unpacked. It was from the "Captain America" series, out of Darrell Jackson's collection. The cover showed Captain America in his red, white, and blue uniform chained to a board, about to be lowered into a caldron of bubbling lava. His captor, the Phoenix ("Who is the Phoenix? You'll GASP—when you learn his SECRET IDENTITY!"), was spraying the room with laser bullets. "You're *too late,* Falcon," the Phoenix told Captain America's sidekick, who had just swung into the chamber on a rope, his cape flying. "TOO LATE! By *LASER BLAST*—or by *molten lava*—Captain America Dies—*now!"* Ordinarily, violent literature is banned from the Kanagy household, and Darrell was enraptured. There was even a 45 rpm record enclosed.

Martha Kanagy distinguishes the two Darrells by calling them by their first and middle names; her son becomes Darrell Lynn and Darrell Jackson is Darrell Christopher. Most of her friends call them White Darrell and Black Darrell—or, just as frequently, Colored Darrell. Darrell Jackson doesn't mind, at least not yet. Although some of his teachers are white, as a practical matter Darrell's world in Brownsville is nearly as segregated as Big Valley, and the subtleties of racial address are dim to him. However, he had given some thought to the nuisance of their identical names.

"Don't you got a nickname or sump'm?" he asked.

"No," said Darrell Kanagy, still buried in the comic book. "Mom says she named me Darrell 'cause it doesn't *have* a nickname. And like everybody I know has one."

"Some of my friends in Brooklyn call me Drill."

"Drill. Hey—that's neat! So, you want me to call you Drill?"

"I don't care."

"No, I got an idea. Let me be Drill."

"Okay. You can be Drill in Pennsylvania, but I'm still Drill in New York."

Martha Kanagy entered the room. "Norm wants you boys to come down and feed the calves."

Neither boy responded.

"What are you reading, Darrell Lynn? Better not let Norm see that! Come on down, he's in the barn. You too, Darrell Christopher."

Darrell Jackson balked. "My momma didn't pay no four dollars for me to have to *work.*"

"Oh, she didn't? Then I hope she sent along plenty of food."

Darrell Jackson laughed and started out the door. Martha looked at her son, deeply involved in the plight of Captain America and pretending to be oblivious. "Darrell Lynn!" Martha warned.

"My name's not Darrell!" he said.

"It's not?"

"It's *snot,*" joked Darrell Jackson.

"It's *Drill.*"

"Only in Pennsylvania," New York Drill reminded him.

Martha put a hand on her hip and smiled to one side —a sardonic gesture she makes when her children catch her off guard. "What's wrong with the name I gave you?"

"I'm *tired* of it, that's all. It's *boring.*"

Martha sighed. "Have you got a new name, too?" she asked Darrell Jackson.

"I was thinkin'. Maybe you could call me D.J."

"Hey, yeah!" said Darrell Kanagy. "D.J. and Drill!"

"Go feed the calves, D.J. and Drill."

Ruth Byler was making butter with an electric churn, a new acquisition she readily appreciated as she could sit in the living room while the machine did its work. Ruth is a hardworking woman with a big voice accustomed to talking over the incidental noises of seven children, but now the house was quiet, except for the hum of the machine and the gulping of the baby at her breast. Ruth wore a purple dress with a pale orange apron, blue tennis shoes, and a pair of black glasses shaped like lemon wedges, darkly shaded for her sensitive eyes. Some of her graying brown hair had begun to leak out the sides of her full Amish covering, giving her a weary, frowzy look. She sang a hymn to the baby, but the nursing and the sound of the churn made her sleepy, and she closed her eyes. Above her on the wall was a picture of Jesus. In the rest of the room there were a china cabinet, a maroon chair and matching couch, plastic flowers in abundance, and bookcases full of Daniel's books.

For an Amishman, Daniel Byler has a rather large library, which he accumulated through membership in The Word Book Club in Waco, Texas. In the case beside his reading chair are books on psychology and counsel-

ing (from a Christian perspective) as well as on theology
—notably, the works of Dietrich Bonhoeffer. Another
case is full of the white-bound *World Book Encyclopedia;*
Daniel says he bought the set for his children, but he
reads it far more than they. The best-thumbed book on
his shelf is a popular paperback on the Second Coming
called *The Late Great Planet Earth,* by Hal Lindsey, which
Daniel Byler considers particularly helpful in understanding the religious schisms in the valley. "There are
pre-millenarians and ante-millenarians," he explains.
"The pre-millenarians believe that the church will become raptured from the world during a seven-year period of tribulation, followed by a thousand-year reign of
Christ on Earth; the ante-millenarians think that events
will happen much more quickly, not spread out over a
thousand years. I'm a pan-millenarian, myself. I believe
things will all pan out in the end."

Daniel jokes about his bookishness, but he suffers a lot
of kidding from his Amish brethren. It is a way of warning him that too much reading can be a sign of worldly
curiosity. Standard fare for an Amishman in the valley are
the Bible and *The Budget,* a weekly newspaper published
in Sugarcreek, Ohio, that consists almost entirely of family news and weather reports from the Amish and Mennonite settlements in North and South America. A
farmer may subscribe to a journal, such as *Holstein/Fri-
sian World,* and he may keep a copy of *Baer's Almanac* at
hand. For news he reads *The Valley Observer,* which ap-
pears every Tuesday with crop reports, results of the
horseshoe-pitching contest, ribbon winners at the youth
fair, hospital admissions and discharges, obituaries, and
supermarket ads from the IGA. World events have no
forum in the Amishman's house, except as signposts of
the Apocalypse.

As a boy Daniel Byler was a member of an Old Order

church, one of the black-buggy groups, and like many who have made the break to a "higher" church Daniel appreciates the new conveniences: the car, the appliances, the electric tools he uses in his work (he fabricates aluminum doors and storm windows in a converted chicken coop near Allensville). At the same time, he laments living in the modern age. "I was born a century too late," he often complains. The happiest period in his life was the two years he spent with his wife and children at a Mennonite mission in Red Lake, Ontario, ministering to the Indians. It gave him the feeling of what it must have been like to be a homesteader on the Western frontier, on the edge of the wilderness, where life is not safe and domesticated. Sometimes he threatens to sell his business and move his family to Alaska—"the last place for folks like me"—and he keeps a map of Alaska on the wall of his bedroom just so Ruth will know he's serious.

What Ruth remembers about the two years in Red Lake is the time Rose almost drowned. She was only four, and fell off the end of a dock into the cold Canadian water. Neither Ruth nor Daniel can swim, so Daniel stretched out on the end of the dock and reached for his daughter's flailing hand. Anna Louise stood behind him, screaming. At that moment Daniel didn't feel very well equipped to live in the wilderness. Fortunately, he caught Rose's hand and pulled her to safety. Rose doesn't even remember the episode, but her sister Anna Louise will never forget it. "Oh, I felt so compassionate—is that the right word? I just held her little hand, and her little tennis shoes were wet and went *squish, squish, squish.*"

Daniel keeps a close watch on the influences to which his children are exposed. Anna Louise and Rose read only inspirational works of Daniel's choosing, although he sometimes gives them books about Eskimos and life in Alaska, which he considers "educational." His oldest son, Elmer, has asked to read the Hardy Boys, but the only detective stories Daniel permits are the Danny Orlis series, in which the protagonist is a Christian. "Why, don't *you* read the Hardy Boys books yourself over in the Lewistown library?" Ruth asked when the subject came up. Daniel admitted that he did, a little surprised and chagrined that his wife had found out. "So, it's okay for you but not for your son," she chided. "I guess that's right," Daniel said. He didn't see a contradiction. It is his responsibility to care for his children's souls until they are baptized, or for as long as they stay in his house. If they want to read the Hardy Boys they can wait till they grow up, as he did.

Daniel gave studied consideration to the decision to invite a Fresh Air child. Ruth's family had Fresh Air children every summer when she was growing up—she still corresponds with one of the girls who visited her— and she argued that the experience couldn't have been *too* corrupting or she wouldn't have lived up to his high standards. Daniel smiled at the sarcasm. With his wife and children all in favor of sending for a child, Daniel gave in, although in truth he was halfway disposed to do it anyway. Fifty weeks out of the year he spends in the company of people who look alike, talk alike, and think alike. A little variety would be welcome—and has been, for the six years that Macy has been coming.

Daniel has a prominent ruddy face with a large, arching forehead, big cheekbones, and a strong chin. His hair is brown, and only his beard is graying. He has unusually shiny eyes. Anna Louise has his eyes and Rose, the more adventurous, has his chin. He is a good-looking man. When he is caught up in his thoughts, as he often is, his expression is amused, with a slight smile. This is how he looked now as he stood inside the screen door (which he had made himself), watching Macy Mizell and his children play games in the yard.

When the stars came out, and it was dark enough, the children played Boogy Bear. The person who was "it" ran and hid while the rest of the children stood on the porch in front of Daniel, counting to twenty. They were sweaty and their clothes were covered with grass stains. At twenty, they marched off the porch chanting, *"There aren't any Boogy Bears out tonight. My grandpappy shot them all last night!"* Suddenly there was a unanimous scream as the Boogy Bear leaped out of hiding. Anna Louise liked to be it, so she often let herself be caught. The rest made it back to the porch, giggling excitedly. They played the game for forty minutes as Daniel watched with undiminished interest.

Finally Ruth called them in for a snack. They sat at the table and sang "God Is Great" before eating cheese curls and pretzels, which they dipped in hot chocolate.

"Well, Macy, do you find anything different this year?" Daniel asked.

"Yeah. What happened to your cow? Where's Peg?"

"Why, Peg's in the freezer," said Ruth.

Macy looked stricken.

"You just now had her in hamburgers for supper," Ruth told her.

Macy leaned back with a nauseated expression and gripped her stomach. "I just ate a cow! I'm gonna be sick!"

"Macy, you knew that hamburgers came from cows!" Ruth said through the general laughter.

"No, I didn't. I knew that they came from beef, but I didn't know that was a cow! I thought beef came from a pig."

Anna Louise clutched her side and laughed, with tears

spilling down her cheeks. "Oh, Macy! You always give me a sideache from laughing too much!"

"I'm eating cows all the time!" Macy realized. "From the time I was a baby—that was more than ten years ago —I musta ate over two cows!"

"Well, do you like sausage, too?" Elmer asked.

"Yeah," said Macy, cautiously, her lip already curling.

"You know the skin on the outside . . . ?"

"It's made from guts!" said Rose, gleefully.

"*AAAAghhh!*" Macy screamed, as she toppled backward in her chair.

Daniel's big laughs filled the house.

Supper sat on the table while everyone waited for Tyrone to get out of the bathroom. He finally appeared and presented his hands to Esther for inspection. "They're cleaner than Galen's," she pronounced. Tyrone smiled and reached for the applesauce.

"We say the blessing first," said Kore.

Tyrone dropped his hands into his lap.

"Father, we want to thank you for bringing rain to the farmers this week," Kore began. "We thank you for this bountiful meal that you've set before us. Especially we want to thank you for bringing Tyrone Howard to join us today from New York. Help us during his stay to be in good fellowship. In Jesus' name. Amen."

Tyrone poured a glass of tea from a plastic pitcher and spiced it with four spoonsful of sugar. He loaded his plate with applesauce, pot roast, potatoes, macaroni salad, and homemade white bread, noticing that the food arrived in familiar plastic containers. He salted everything liberally, including the applesauce. At the end of the table were potato chips, also in a plastic container. "You a Tupperware dealer?" he asked Esther.

Esther was astonished. "How did you know?"

"My muvver, she was. They give her the Butterfly Award."

"The which?"

"The woman with the butterfly wings."

"You mean the angel?"

"Yeah."

"She must've been a manager," Esther concluded. "Did she show you how to burp the seals, then?"

Tyrone nodded. "And she gimme fifty cents to unpack the boxes."

"Fifty cents, yet!" Galen complained. "I only got a dime!"

Kore changed the subject. "What sort of work does your father do?"

"He deliver telephone books."

"Oh, that's interesting."

"You got a job?" asked Tyrone.

Kore smiled at the presumption that he might *not* have a job. The only unemployed person he had ever heard of in the valley is Froggy McPhee, the Belleville derelict, who lives on welfare and spends his days drinking beer and watching the traffic go by. Froggy is locally famous because of his frequent mention in sermons devoted to the evils of alcohol. Whenever anyone talks about unemployment as a national problem, Kore thinks of Froggy sitting on the curb with a can of beer in his hand. "I'm a carpenter," Kore told Tyrone.

"I got jobs too," said Tyrone. "Eleben."

"Eleven jobs?"

"Uh-huh. I works in a barbershop. I picks up hair. Sometime I hole the kids so they can get they hair cut. And I clean lady houses. That's my different jobs. My udder jobs is reading and gardening."

"That's fine," said Esther. "I think your parents

must've raised you right. I'd like to meet them sometime, especially your mother—I don't wonder we'd have a lot to talk about!"

Tyrone grinned.

"Do you have any brothers and sisters?" Janet asked.

"I got nine," said Tyrone. "Four bruvvers and five sisters. I had twenty-two, but the rest died."

"Oh, Tyrone!" Esther laughed nervously.

"You don't b'leeb me?"

"I didn't say that—"

"How old is your mother?" asked Janet.

"She elderly. Thirty-nine. No, thirty-eight. I forget."

"Do they all live with you?"

"The live ones do," said Tyrone. "We got sixteen in the house, if you be countin' my sister' babies and my gran'muvver. She not my real gran'muvver. She my foster gran'muvver."

"So your mother was a Tupperware dealer," Esther remarked, trying to put a rudder in the drift of conversation, which seemed to be headed for some dreadful niagara.

"Uh-huh. But robbers broke in the basement and stole it all."

"Stole the Tupperware," Esther said hopelessly.

"They musta had a truck! It was in *Brooklyn*," Tyrone explained.

"Oh, you'uns live in Brooklyn, then?" asked Kore.

"Not me, Jack. I live in Queens!"

"Queens," Janet repeated, relishing the royal sound. "I wonder what it's like to live in Queens?"

"It's nice," Tyrone admitted. "They raise lots of things, and they got bigger yards than here. They got apple trees and cherry trees and big watermelon patches in people's backyards."

"And that's different from Brooklyn, yet?" asked Janet.

"In Brooklyn you get a free lunch," Tyrone informed her. "Everybody. Sometime they get breakfast in the morning, and a whole big cartful of lunch. Any place you see a big line, you get a apple, at least."

"I wish I could go to Brooklyn!" Janet looked at her mother. *"Some* people won't even let me go to Lewistown."

"The only thing you see in Brooklyn is dead people," Tyrone warned her. "This man got shot off the roof with a cannon! No, not a cannon—a bazooka!"

Galen's mouth was wide open. "A bazooka!"

"People die in their apartments! I stay in the house behind double-double-double locks. I don't wanna die."

"How awful!" Janet clapped her hand over her mouth.

For dessert there was ice cream and potato chips and a shoofly cake made with brown sugar and molasses. Tyrone had two slices.

After supper, Galen and Janet cleaned the kitchen and the dining room while Tyrone helped Esther wash the dishes—his regular chore at home, he told her. "I even brought my Vaseline Intensive Care for my hands. Soap gonna dry out your skin. Sometime I use grease. I puts it on my hands and face."

"Grease!" said Esther.

"It's good for you. You oughtta try it."

The telephone rang and Esther answered it. "Oh, hello, Mrs. Howard . . ." she said. "Yes, Tyrone's here. I must say, he is *so* well behaved!"

Tyrone smiled.

"He is?" asked Mrs. Howard in a puzzled tone on the other end of the line.

"Yes, he's a great help."

"Axe her didn't she have twenty-two babies!"

"What's that boy sayin'?" asked Mrs. Howard.

"He, uh—"

"Ma!" Tyrone hollered, "she don't b'leeb you got twenty-two babies!"

"Oh," said Mrs. Howard. "He never gets that right. What he means is I was pregnant twenty-two times."

"Really? That's—um. Amazing."

"Didn't I tole you!" Tyrone bragged.

"Ten babies and twelve miscarriages," Mrs. Howard explained. "One thing about Tyrone: he don't always get it right, but he never tell a lie. None of my children lie."

Esther handed the phone to Tyrone and sat weakly at the kitchen table.

"Hi, Ma!" Tyrone said happily. "Did gran'muvver get her leg?"

# Chapter 5

Tyrone lives in the Jamaica section of Queens, in an exhausted, weather-eaten cottage tinted, like most of the houses on his block, in faded postwar pastels of orange and lime. It is not a shantytown, not yet. The houses are clapboard cousins evenly spaced for block after block like a military cantonment, prefabricated and never meant to last, with trees and sidewalks and unattended shrubbery turning to riot. Although Jamaica shares most of the problems of New York's slums, Pauline Howard considers it an improvement over the other places they've lived. She often reminds her children to be grateful they're no longer living in Brooklyn.

Tyrone shares the top bunk in one upstairs bedroom with a younger brother; two other brothers sleep in the bunk below. The room is embellished with comic-book pages taped to the walls, and dirty handprints on the woodwork. There is a considerable hole in the ceiling, marking the spot where Tyrone's older brother fell through the floor of the attic. From the bedroom window the boys can watch the neighbor lady undress. She stands right in view, perfectly aware of the giggling noises and the little heads peeking over the windowsill.

The house in summer is an oven; in the winter it is so drafty that one's hair moves in the breeze. In November the boys move into their parents' room, with their sisters and their sisters' children, fifteen people in all, as many as possible in the same bed trying to get warm. The radiator is scorching but pathetically ineffective against the Siberian gusts that blow through the house. The Howards huddle together in the master bedroom with a color TV and a refrigerator beside the bed, so that on really cold mornings they don't have to venture downstairs at all, except to check on Tyrone's foster grandmother, an amputee, who waits month after month in the front room of the Howards' house for her artificial limb to arrive.

James Howard, Tyrone's father, doesn't work. He complains of gastritis, hypertension, and lower-back pains, and hopes soon to claim a disability from Social Security. Until then, the Howard family receives $884 a month in welfare payments, an amount that is augmented by food stamps, tax exemptions, Medicaid, and odd jobs on the sly—mainly, delivering telephone books for the New York Telephone Company. (The family breaks into two crews, one to each car, with James and Pauline doing the chauffeuring and the boys delivering the books.) In a year's time the Howard family may actually spend more money than Galen Peachey's family, but they get comparatively little for it. Their worn-out house in Queens rents for $350 a month; for the same amount in Big Valley they could lease a seventy-acre farm with a much larger and much sturdier house.

Pauline Howard, a robust, convivial woman, was raised on a farm in South Carolina, and she sends her children through the Fresh Air Fund so that they can learn country values. "The main problem in the city is keeping them with the right class of children. I didn't have that problem when I was growing up. Now I have to teach them how to defend theirselves, get along in the city. Like Tyrone, he *always* getting into trouble. He wants to be the boss. He gets the devil in him and he wants to fight. Sometimes I have to box Tyrone like I box a man."

Tyrone is a loner. He doesn't trust people, not even his family. In school he has the reputation of being a bully, which he enjoys. "I boss 'em all," he brags. "Kindergarten too." His mother has warned him, "If you ever go in a gang, don't come to me no more." Tyrone is such a solipsist that the idea of joining a gang never occurred to him; he forms his own, ad hoc. "At the other school [in Brooklyn] I used to have six, seven gangs. At my next school I have a lot more gangs. Better gangs. And when I have 'em, it'll be more fightin'. More better. More people who can fight, and defend themself. If they don't defend themself they gonna be beat up, long as they live." In fact, Tyrone himself almost never fights. He engineers a conflict, then quickly retreats, complaining of an upset stomach.

In his spare time Tyrone breaks into abandoned houses. The neighborhood is full of them. Many are burned out and dangerous. Sometimes he stumbles upon snoring winos. Once, one of them woke up, scaring himself and Tyrone so badly that the wino fell down the steps and Tyrone jumped out the window.

Tyrone's brothers think he is crazy, but they admire the loot he brings home. Cleon, Tyrone's older brother, remembers "cats, dogs, flashlights, toys, baby carriages, money, a radio, a little camera, books, watches, money, a ten-speed bike . . ." He calls Tyrone "a prehistoric kid" —a scavenger on the land. Everyone admits Tyrone has a genius for finding things. He is always the first to spot a nickel on the sidewalk. Once he found a wallet containing $20.51. He found a cache of sex books and got a fast education. "I thought it wasn't even *real* before I saw it in the book!" Another time he discovered a half-full druggist's bottle with a skull and crossbones on the front. He brought it home and set it on the dresser. His mother found it before he got it open—a bottle of arsenic.

"The other day he even found fleas in a house," jokes Cleon. "He was full of fleas when he came home." That's the only thing Cleon remembers that Tyrone ever shared with everybody else. His brothers describe him as "mean and stingy," and "hardheaded." "He's bad, in lots of ways," says Cleon. "One time I had a gardening job and got sick, and I let Tyrone go in my place. Tyrone took it away from me. That's the way he is."

Tyrone smiles. "You don't got friends in this world, you got enemies," is his philosophy. "The people you think is you friends is you enemies. I got enemies everywhere."

Ann Peachey, the Fresh Air chairperson, telephoned Esther Peachey, her sister-in-law.

"Esther? Just checking on your Fresh Air. What's his name . . . ?"

"Tyrone? A handful, all right! He just won't left Galen alone. Soon's I thought they were getting along good, this forenoon they had a squabble. Tyrone was holding a porkypine quill and he stuck it clear through Galen's jeans right into his butt, yet. Galen jumped back and said, 'You dumb queer!' Had to pull it out himself, it was that far in! Tyrone said it was an 'accident.' I just didn't know what to do!"

"What did you do then?"

"Why, I left him know what it felt like! I gave him a poke, kinda, and then he sulked all through dinner and wouldn't touch his food. I sent them over to Norm's to play till supper. How's your Luke getting on with Franklin this year?"

"Oh, they're doing fine. Franklin lost his Afro pick on the bus, and he said he just had to have a new one. Can you imagine trying to buy an Afro pick in Big Valley? I told him I really didn't know where to find one. I'm not even sure they have any in Lewistown, yet. He said, 'Mom, I can't use a regular comb. Couldn't we please go to the store and look?' So I took him to the White Hall store and I was so surprised. He says, 'Mom, they do too have Afro picks!' Know what they were? Cake cutters, the metal kind with the long tines. Franklin says it's better than his old one!"

"Well, I hope we don't have any firebugs this year."

"Already, we have. Leonard's girl."

"Leonard Zook's!"

"Set fire to the mattress."

"Are they sending her back, then?"

"No, Leonard's Bertha wants to give her another chance, yet."

"She has that much love in her heart!"

# Chapter 6

Sunday. A procession of black cars rolled funereally through Belleville and accumulated like a storm cloud in the parking lot of the Laurel Hill Amish Church. The autos, all black as tar, ranged from luxurious Oldsmobiles to self-effacing Comets and Vegas. Dorcas Swarey's Volkswagen is the only foreign car in the congregation. It has less than 24,000 miles on it after ten years of operation, and is still running on its original tires.

Daniel Byler wheeled into the lot in a 1970 Dodge Polara. As a driver he is a menace, for he refuses to wear his glasses. Anna Louise and Rose don't know what his prescription is, only that it's worse than their mother's (and she's often said that without her glasses she can't see across the room). It's a minor conceit among the men of the Laurel Hill Church to refuse to wear glasses until they are elderly or virtually blind. Macy Mizell linked arms with Rose and followed the rest of the Byler clan out of the morning heat.

The cornfields skirting the windows of the church rippled in the mirrory sheen of shellac on the blond wood pews. The center aisle, dividing the men from the women, was a gray linoleum waxed to such a gloss that it seemed to puddle in sunlit pools, like a highway mirage. At the end of the aisle was a bench of preachers dressed in black, five of them, black beards on the flanks, gray inside and white in the middle, this last wearing a pair of unrimmed spectacles which caught the light like two silver dollars. Above him on the whitewashed wall was an octagonal clock with a silver pendulum ticking audibly toward nine o'clock. At his feet, like a holy ornament in the very center of the dais, was a single white electrical outlet.

Macy ignored the inquisitive stares and entered haughtily in an apple-green sleeveless blouse and dark green culottes, her favorite outfit for Mass. She felt horribly singular nevertheless and looked about for the only other Fresh Air in her church—but when she spotted Natasha Brown, her mouth dropped open. Not only was Natasha wearing an Amish dress, she was also wearing a white devotional covering. Which meant that Macy was the only girl in church without one! She shot Natasha a murderous look; Natasha shrank in her seat. Macy and Rose sat three rows up on the far side of the pew.

This year Natasha had mixed feelings about "dressing Dutch." When she sees Macy Mizell in her pretty culottes, or playing with the Byler girls in rainbow jeans or even shorts, Natasha wishes that Dorcas would let her wear her own clothes. On the other hand, with her heightened sense of style Natasha knows that the long dress favors her figure, and with the deep maroon color against her dark skin, her almond-shaped Polynesian eyes, and her hair gleaming in tight braids under the bright white covering—she seems the essence of glamour. And that, of course, is the very opposite of the effect intended by the prim Amish dress.

After the adults and children were settled, the unmarried girls streamed in, occupying the front two pews in a long line of white organdy pinafores and black devotional coverings. (They wear this contrasting attire until their wedding day, when the black covering is changed for white and the pinafore is set aside until their burial.) Anna Louise Byler, who would turn twelve this week, was wearing the black covering for the first time. She cast an excited smile as she passed by, which Macy returned and Rose refused to notice. On the opposite side, their heavy shoes thundering on the linoleum like horses on a bridge, the eligible boys clumped in, filling the church with self-importance and the smell of soap.

A man up front called out a number in German and the congregation sang from the *Ausbund,* the collection of sixteenth-century hymns of the Anabaptist martyrs. Amish hymns resemble the Gregorian chants of the Latin liturgy, but they are slower and cast in a heavily minor key, so that they sound pentatonic and mournful, unrelieved by harmony or accompaniment. Each syllable is at least a whole note or as much as a full measure—it's impossible to say, since the *Ausbund* has no score, only lyrics in a Gothic script. Natasha held the heavy book in her lap and mouthed voicelessly—"lip singing," she calls it, "like on 'Soul Train.' "

Singing styles are dogma in the valley churches. Four verses of the Amish anthem, *Lobelied,* which is always the second hymn sung in an Amish church, take nearly fifteen minutes in the Laurel Hill Church. In the Old Order churches they may take over twenty minutes. Sunday evenings, Amish teenagers often gather for singing, and then they may sing Protestant hymns, sometimes in English; but even then the tempo is slowed to a dirge. Mennonites sing faster, and they harmonize expertly. The Mennonite hymnal is scored with shape notes, so that the congregation can anticipate the consonance without an organ to show them the way. There is almost no secular music in the valley, other than children's play songs. Those Mennonites who own a record player mainly enjoy gospel music recorded by groups such as the Inspirations and the Happy Goodman Family. Soloists are disapproved of. Symphonic music, opera, jazz, blues, rock—the whole scale of musical expression—are all just "noises" to the ears of the pious. As much could be said of literature or painting. Secular art, above the level of handicrafts, does not exist in Amish-Mennonite culture.

Natasha scanned the singing congregation. The men had their hair shaved in back level with their earlobes, so that the cords of their necks bristled like those of young boys. One of the men stared back, and abruptly his mouth popped open as if he were going to scream. It turned into a huge yawn. Amish people, Natasha contends, never cover their mouths when they yawn.

The rear pews on the left were full of mothers with their uncommonly silent infants. Amish children are soon taught to sit quietly for long periods of time, with nothing more to divert them than a plain white handkerchief, which they twist and fold and tie, then smooth out again on their laps. If the child gets rambunctious the mother may use the kerchief as a gag, until he settles down or falls asleep. Natasha was surprised to see one of the children carrying a doll—a little Amish doll dressed in white, with a long oval face and slightly yellow coloring, like antique china. Suddenly the doll moved, and Natasha nearly jumped out of her seat. It was the smallest human thing Natasha had ever seen, a midget girl, who began to play with a handkerchief and nervously avoided Natasha's stare. Natasha felt Dorcas Swarey poke her in the side, and she turned around.

The white-bearded preacher with the shiny spectacles stood up to deliver the first sermon. He spoke in a sing-song voice, in German, tediously rotating from side to side, raising one arm up, then down, then the other, on and on, on and on, like a toy drummer with an inexhaustible spring. Natasha moved her head in syncopation with the preacher's lugubrious cadence. Her eyes drifted up to the octagonal clock and stuck on the swinging silver pendulum. In a moment she was gone, transported from the stark Amish meetinghouse to the Deliverance Tabernacle in Bedford-Stuyvesant . . .

There the young pastor stands framed in roses on the stage of an old movie theater, with a towering chrome cross where the screen used to be, lit in a red blaze. The Supernatural Voices of Deliverance are singing and swinging and the organ player mops his face with a silk bandanna. Franklin Williams is there, handsome and stylish in his baby-blue French suit, and he smiles at Natasha as he passes the silver collection plate. She is on her feet, waving her arms in a garden of bonnets, and the people around her are jumping up and down and shouting hallelujahs and praising the name of the Lord. Sometimes the Spirit comes into a brother or sister so mightily that a person loses control and begins to thrash and speak in tongues. Then a group of women dressed like nurses surrounds him and they link arms, to keep him from hurting himself; and inside that circle of starched white bosoms he flails and howls until the Spirit lets up and leaves him spent, and he sinks into the white arms. The jubilation is always at its pitch when the pastor comes down from the stage and the healing line forms, winding along a wall that is decorated with discarded canes and walkers, which hang like trophies on a long metal rail.

Once Natasha stood in the healing line to see what it

would be like. The pastor held out his palm to the man behind him, who squirted it with olive oil from a plastic ketchup bottle. Then, as the people in front of Natasha approached, with their hands in surrender and singing out hallelujahs, the pastor would slap the oil on their brows and rattle their heads—you could see the charge jolting through their quivering hands. Natasha was glad that didn't happen to her. "He just put oil on my head. He don't slap the kids." At times the pastor snatches the ketchup bottle and squirts a long stream into a communicant's mouth, until the person's knees go limp and the nurse-like women catch him and lead him to a seat. Natasha has seen the sick healed and the lame made to walk freely again, but she still recalls what happened to her friend Margaret. "She in a wheeling chair, and they prayed over her, and she *still* in a wheeling chair."

When the light flashes ON THE AIR, the congregation subsides and the elegant young pastor of Deliverance Tabernacle rises to the podium and begins his sermon: "Hide Not What Ye Believe," taken from the fourth chapter of II Corinthians. "I was on a bus," says the pastor, "and one of these young girls was readin' the *National Enquirer*"—Natasha gulps, for she reads *every issue*—"and it seemed like she knew everything about those movie stars. But she didn't know nothin' about the Spirit of God!"

*"Say it now!"* the congregation responds.

"She was hiding what she believes! Readin' that trash, wearin' a halter top, listenin' to that rock and roll music—"

*"Watch out! You tell it!"*

"She was letting the world take over! You look aroun' and what you see? Boys lookin' like girls! You can't tell 'em apart! Turn on the TV and watch a so-called family show, it's sex and violence and ugly language ruinin' our young people's minds. They don't care if you likes it 'cause they ain't hidin' nothin' no more!"

*"Nothin'! Thass right!"*

"People are ashamed. They are hiding their godliness. They are letting the world take over! It's taking over our minds, our bodies, our clothes—they even playin' rock and roll music in the church!"

*"Yeow! Well, well!"*

"Letting the world take over! You can ride aroun' all day in you big ol' Mercedes-Benz automobile and that don't mean nothin'! 'Cause on the last day you be seein' God or the Devil—and they don't take trade-ins!"

*"Lord! He's sayin' it now!"*

"This is the late edition! Hot off the press! If you 'shamed of Jesus, pack up you bag and go back to business! If you 'shamed of Jesus, you ain't never gonna stand with Him when He come for his bride, hallelujah!"

*"Hallelujah!"*

As Natasha napped, virtually the same sermon was being delivered by a graybeard in the Laurel Hill Church, his false teeth punctuating each homily with a moist click. By now the congregation was swimming in fatigue, like fogbound travelers in the airport of a small town. Dorcas Swarey sat sternly upright and listened dutifully to the sermon, her face registering an opinion on every statement the preacher made, approving nods or displeased scowls, so that he gradually began to fix on her. His eyes would sweep over the heads of the sleepy worshippers, avoiding the contagion of their yawns; then quickly check the impression he had made on Dorcas's face; then pass on; then back again, as if she were gravity itself and he were the pendulum on the wall behind him.

Dorcas has that effect. She is not pretty. Her face is pale, but frank and full of certainty.

There is no graceful role for the unmarried woman in Amish society, which is structured on family life and is almost incapable of defining adulthood outside of marriage. Although Dorcas suffered from acne and her physique was too bony by Amish standards, she was surprised to find herself at the age of twenty-nine still sitting in the front of the church with the virgins in their white pinafores and black coverings, while her peers sat in the back tending to children. After all of her younger sisters were married Dorcas realized she would never be asked. Since she couldn't expect to live in her father's house forever, she took up housekeeping for her brother Ezra. For a year she continued to wear the black covering and sit with the teenaged girls. Finally she just appeared one Sunday dressed as an adult, and sat in the back among the white coverings of her friends. She was carrying a three-month-old foster child who was "biracial."

Brother Ezra was embarrassed; he refused to take responsibility for the baby. "I don't think he ever even dressed her for church," Dorcas recalls. "He wasn't interested in children at all until he had his own."

When Ezra married, Dorcas had to move off the farm and fend for herself. "Living alone wasn't my choice. It was really the last resort." She hung a hand-painted motto on her wall: NEVER BE AFRAID TO ENTRUST AN UNKNOWN FUTURE TO A KNOWN GOD. She thought she saw what the Lord had in mind for her: to adopt children, and spend on them the love that could find no other outlet. She tried to adopt her foster child, but the welfare agency said her income was inadequate and took the child away. Dorcas hung out a sign saying BAKED GOODS FOR SALE, and made bread every day, and half-moon pies and ginger cookies and jelly rolls. It helped, but it was only a marginal business in a valley where most women baked their own bread and pastries. She had to give it up anyway when the welfare office sent her a three-year-old retarded child named Karen, who couldn't talk or even walk on her own. After Karen there was another child, a pretty biracial boy with coffee-colored skin, named Peter. Within a year, Dorcas tried to adopt him, but her income was still too small and then Peter was gone. All she had now was Natasha, for two weeks in the summer.

This year when Natasha came she learned that Dorcas had a new profession. The living room was full of heavy bolts of black cloth. "I'm a tailor, now," Dorcas explained, pointing to a box of orders beside her sewing machine that would take her months to fill. "Next time I ask to adopt a child, I'm thinking they won't be turning me down."

Once while Dorcas was braiding her hair Natasha asked her if she'd like a little girl of her own. Dorcas was working Natasha's hair into an Amish-style "French curl," with a long braid on each side drawn into a bun in back. Natasha, in turn, was braiding the blond nylon hair of her "doll baby" into tight corn rows.

"I like to help other little children who need me."

"But don't you want one of your *own?*"

"If I was to be married, yes."

"You don't gotta be *married!* My momma got three babies and she ain't never been married."

"Wouldn't you want her to be?"

"Yea-ah," Natasha admitted. "My father begged my momma to marry him but she wouldn't 'cause she too young."

Dorcas coated the braids with Vaseline to make them

shine, a trick she had learned from Natasha. "Perhaps someday they will."

"He found another lady, and now he have a daughter name Sharon. When he come over I axe him why you never bring Sharon? 'Cause that's half my sister."

Dorcas and Natasha often discuss religion—it's something they have in common, and Natasha is relentless on subjects she thinks they share—but as they talk, it occurs to Dorcas that the very things they seem to agree upon actually disguise unbridgeable chasms. Natasha is a devout child, but she frets about not having been baptized. The rite of baptism at Deliverance Tabernacle (as Natasha describes it) involves a tank of water, "and the preacher back you up to it and duck you head under the water for a couple a hours. I mean a couple a minutes." Dorcas heard the apprehension in her voice and assured her that there are other means of baptism—such as pouring, as they do in the Amish church—which are not so threatening. "But I never even been in the preacher' arms!" Natasha moaned. The image made Dorcas giggle. "I never was in a preacher's arms either," she said in the spiraling nervous titter that overtakes her when she thinks of men.

"I was s'posed to get baptize way back, but I haven't a white gown," Natasha lamented. "And you know what my brother say? I was gonna get baptize in the *gutter.*"

"In the gutter!"

"Yea-ah! With the johnny pump on!"

Actually, Natasha has secretly contrived to put off her baptism several times. For her, baptism is salvation, and in Natasha's mind being saved means surrendering certain pleasures she's loath to part with, such as dancing and rock and roll music. It also represents a revolt against her mother, or her mother's way of life, and Natasha is still too terrified of going to Heaven if it means her mother will be going to Hell without her. In New York, Natasha often brings home prayer cards from church requesting that her mother be saved, and she leaves them around the house so that they are easily noticed. Her mother wonders how much of this proselytizing comes from Deliverance Tabernacle, and how much is inspired by Dorcas.

The truth is that Natasha's confident talk of salvation makes Dorcas uneasy as well. In her church the idea of knowing that you are saved, of being born again, is heresy. One can only live a proper life and hope for the best. Amish baptism is less a religious rite than a cultural one, signifying that a person subscribes to the Amish way of life and thought and that future deviance may be punished by excommunication and shunning. Dorcas has seen it happen in her own church. The Amish do not baptize children because they are innocents.

Just before noon, the elderly bishop unfolded from the amen corner to deliver his testimony, and Dorcas wakened Natasha with a gentle shake of her shoulders. When the bishop finished, the worshippers wheeled about in a unanimous movement and knelt on the floor with their heads in the pews, praying silently. Then they rose at once and church was over.

Afterward, people stood around and chatted before the business meeting, which was open only to members. Daniel Byler greeted several men friends with a kiss on the mouth—the holy kiss, or kiss of charity, mentioned in Romans 16:16. The first time Macy saw him do it she was scandalized.

The children fled outside. Macy tried to get the attention of Irene Peight, the midget, who kept averting her glances—so that Macy tried to make it into a game of peekaboo. Irene was so fragile and beautiful, like some incalculably valuable object, that Macy wanted desperately to hold her and was frustrated that her advances seemed so frightening. "You look such a giant to her, Macy!" Anna Louise reminded her. Macy agreed. "If she was to be in a crowd, she'd get crushed! Somebody'd step on her for sure!"

When Natasha came out, barefoot and waltzy, Macy was still ignoring her. Natasha didn't mind. She descended into a circle of girls dressed in purple and blue and sitting in the shade. They were singing hymns. In a moment they were laughing at Natasha's attempt at *"Wo ist Jesus, mein Verlangen,"* which Natasha knew as "What a Friend We Have in Jesus." The little girl who was carrying Irene Peight in her arms came over and sat down, and Irene crawled down and sat like a white elf in the thick grass. She was six years old and weighed nine pounds. Her eyes were wide-spaced and intelligent, and her features faultlessly shaped, as anything miniature seems more nearly perfect than its larger model. Irene's singing voice was high and tinkly, like the sound of breaking crystal. She sat with her feet crossed and her hands in her lap and her covering neatly tied below the point of her chin. She and Natasha studied each other slyly, in accidental glances. When the hymn was over she said something in Dutch to her younger sister and the other girls laughed. "She wants you to teach us one of your songs, now," a girl translated to Natasha.

"You know 'Hot Line, Hot Line'?" Natasha asked.

The girls looked at each other and shrugged.

"You ain't know it?" Natasha quickly taught them the chorus:

> *"Hot line, hot line*
> *I'm callin' on the hot line,*
> *On the hot line!"*

Irene spoke English poorly, and she struggled over the words and the strange tune. Natasha was patient. When Dorcas found her, Natasha's breathy contralto was leading the ensemble in a slowed-down approximation of the hit tune, with Natasha's version of the lyrics:

> *"Girl, the way you move your lips*
> *I can't tell you got finer kiss!*
> *The way you blush your eyes*
> *They shine like innocent skies!*
> *Oh baby, baby!*
> *Hot line, hot line!*
> *I'm callin' on the hot line*
> *For your lo-o-ove!"*

# Chapter 7

The girls slept crossways in the double bed with Macy in the middle, her feet hanging six inches over the edge and twitching in the cool breeze from the open window. Macy's weight tended to pull Rose and Anna Louise into the center, so that when Ruth Byler opened the door at 6:30 A.M. she found Macy on the bottom of the heap, her breath coming in husky gasps. The room was ruddy with the sunrise.

Macy dressed in her rainbow jeans and a blue tank top. "You daresn't go barefoot yet," Anna Louise warned her. "Last year I thought you never would stop complaining about your poor feet!"

"They hurt something horrible," Macy agreed. "And you'uns said they might need cutting off!" Already she was talking in the special tune of the valley, a higher-pitched, vaguely interrogatory, Irish sound. It is this intonation that confounds and exasperates Macy's mother when her daughter returns. Macy's Big Valley brogue lasts for more than a week in the city, until she forgets how it goes. But when she returns to the Bylers it is back upon her instantly.

"Last one up has to red up the bed!" Anna Louise called as she and Macy left the room. Rose moaned from under the covers.

"That lazy girl!" said Macy, who was awake a full five hours before she normally rises in the summer in New York.

Morning in the valley is divided into two parts, called morning and forenoon, and they are separated by breakfast. The girls spent the morning mowing the dewy grass and tending the piebald bantam chickens that Anna Louise and Rose raise to sell. "We started with three for my birthday," said Rose. "Now we've got thirty-five!"

The smell of the barn overwhelmed the aroma of freshly cut grass and the breakfast cooking in the kitchen. It was a scratchy dry smell that made Macy's eyes water. On the floor of the barn they found newly hatched "peeps," yellow and still dizzy from birth. Macy cuddled the little chickens in her hands. "That's why I'd like to live up here, 'cause you can get pets for presents." She looked dreamily at the dusty sunlight streaking through the cracked wood. She sneezed.

Samuel, the second-youngest child, hollered something in Dutch from the hayloft.

"What'd that boy say?"

"He found some eggs that didn't hatch," said Anna Louise. "Let's crack 'em open and see what they look like."

"Oooh, no! I got a *very* weak stomach!"

Samuel's blond head appeared in the trap of the loft. "Macy! *Kum de riva!*"

"Not on your life!"

Samuel disappeared. In a moment a small white egg arced through the trap and splattered at Macy's feet. She stared paralyzed at the glistening black embryo, with its yellow beak and white-rimmed eyes. "Get it away! Get it away!"

Anna Louise picked up the embryo by one wing.

"They get feathers in no time!" she observed.

"Should we feed 'em to the pigs, then?" asked Rose.

"I don't know. The pigs ate the rooster and a banty that we had before, already," Anna Louise explained to Macy.

"The pigs! Oh, ugh!"

Elmer came with a bucket to milk the cow. He wiped her teats with a wet rag and then made the bucket ring with jets of milk. The underside of the cow was freckled with black flies that crept across the veins of the heavy udder or settled on the green boots of dung on the animal's hind legs. "Oh, yeccht!" said Macy. "Elmer's standing in the cow maneuver."

Elmer pointed a teat at Macy and spurted hot milk on the front of her blue tank top. Macy kicked him in the chest, and when he stood up she tried to knee him in the groin. Elmer protected himself with both hands and Macy slapped him, knocking his glasses off. Elmer laughed nervously.

"You want to milk her then?" he asked, backing away.

Macy squatted on the stool and looked at the oozing teats, wrinkled and pink. She reached in, then drew her hand away. "I don't wanna touch her there."

Elmer knelt under the cow and put his lips over a teat. His Adam's apple raced up and down his throat as he sucked.

"Children!" Ruth shouted from the house. *"Kum esa!"*

On the breakfast table were large bowls of applesauce and oatmeal, a pan of cornmeal mush, and a platter of eggs, sunnyside up. Above the table hung a fly ribbon studded with victims. Ruth came out of the hot kitchen carrying a pitcher of milk.

"I don't think I'm ready for this," Macy warned. She looked queasy.

"Shhh!" said Rose. They bowed their heads for silent prayer.

The Dutch diet is suspected in the untimely coronaries that depopulate the valley of middle-aged men at a reputedly high rate. Although it is more "natural" than food in the city, in the sense that it is homemade and free of additives, the diet is heavily inclined toward carbohydrates and saturated fats. Sugar is purchased in one-hundred-pound sacks, to be used in canning fruit or in making the multiple desserts that follow most meals, sometimes in several courses. Virtually everyone in the valley has a sweet tooth, and their teeth show it. It doesn't help that their drinking water, drawn directly from a mountain stream, is free not only of fluoride but also of many minerals that help teeth develop. As a consequence the enamel is soft and easy prey for disease. Both Anna Louise and Rose have disfiguring cavities in the front of their mouths, as does their mother. Daniel's teeth are gleamingly white and perfect—like many Amishmen, he had his own pulled before he got married and replaced them with full plates. It is said that the only dentist some Amishmen visit is in South Carolina. He owns an all-night denture clinic which is next to a motel and he promises next-day service. The outfit is abhorred by reputable dentists, who can recognize the plates by their poor craftsmanship and invariably painful fit.

Ruth admired Macy's teeth at the breakfast table. Although one of her front incisors had been broken in a baseball game, Macy has even white teeth and only three fillings. "I guess you don't eat candy, then," said Ruth.

"I sure do!"

"Then you drink a lot of milk, yet."

"We got a dentist what work in our school. Free of charge!"

"Do you? My girls need going pretty bad."

"Oh, Ma, I *hate* going, like anything!" said Rose.

"You daresn't wait too long or he'll be taking them out, yet."

"I've only got three fillings," Macy reminded everyone.

"Well, you've got the fluoride in the water, there in New York," said Daniel. "Did you hear that they think maybe fluoride causes abnormal behavior in children?"

"I ain't crazy!" Macy snapped.

Daniel laughed in big barks, and Macy looked embarrassed.

"It's the milk," Ruth insisted.

A firecracker exploded in the distance, but nobody realized that today was the Fourth of July.

In the creek at the bottom of a steep dirt cliff Galen stirred a mortar of mud and pebbles. He poured it across the mound of heavy stones that his cousin, Luke Peachey, had stacked across the creek bed. The boys stood in the muddied water with their pants rolled up above their knees. Already the water was building behind the dam in a wide pool. Franklin Williams was perfecting an "overflow valve" of pipe and screen. The trees on either bank were attenuated by the long climb to sunlight.

Luke patted the mortar flat with the back of his shovel. He looked up and laughed at the immobilized figure of Tyrone Howard standing ten feet away in water over his knees. "Hey, Tyrone!" No response.

Tyrone was staring up through a dappled canopy of waving leaves, spellbound, his hand stuck deep in his mouth. His upper right molar. He couldn't leave it alone. All morning he had played with it in the bathroom and now the tooth was so loose that he could almost lift it out—except for a single aching root which always tugged it back. Tyrone had a headache from missing breakfast and was growing nauseated from the taste of blood on an empty stomach. *When the vampire drink you blood it's like tomato soup,* he decided, just as Luke poured a bucket of water over his head.

Tyrone roared into the pool, wheeling and splashing. He grabbed Franklin's bucket (Franklin had fled to the higher bank) and sloshed it out with Galen and Luke. It was no match. He chased them both out of the pond and captured their buckets, then stood dripping and laughing at his victory. His ribs heaved through his soaking tee shirt.

From the bank Franklin called for time. A few stones had worked loose during the fight and parts of the over-flow valve were floating downstream. "Hey, let me work on the dam, Tyrone!"

"You come down here, Jack, and I'll work on you head!"

Galen and Luke giggled. They were sneaking around Tyrone from either side. Galen's foot slipped in a fresh green patty of "cow poo."

Tyrone's lip curled. "I smell a cow!"

"You smell yourself!" Galen hurled the turd at Tyrone's back. From the other side Luke grabbed a bucket and the battle resumed. Water flew in enormous chaos. "Hey, don't get me wet!" Franklin cried from the bank above.

"C'mon and play!" said Luke.

"Okay, but I'm gonna be on Tyrone's side," said Franklin. "It's gonna be New Yorkers versus country."

"Then I quit," said Galen. "King's X." He turned away from Tyrone and got a full bucketload against the back of his head.

"Ain't no times out, sucker."

Galen's lips formed a crooked pout. He climbed the bank where Franklin was still sitting and found Tyrone's Roman sandals and tossed them into the pool, then ran into the woods and hid. Tyrone filled a bucket and charged after him.

"You wanna fight, Jack?" Tyrone shouted into the foliage. Tyrone shook the thin trees as if Galen would plop out of one, like a coconut.

Galen reappeared under the lip of the bank, just below Franklin's feet. He peered over the grass and saw Tyrone racing through the woods in crazy circles, spewing water. Galen's pale skin was drawn into gooseflesh. "Hey, Franklin," he whispered, "why don't you get Tyrone?"

Franklin shrugged helplessly. "I'd like to, Galen, but he's on my *side.*"

Galen ran back into the creek with Luke. When he turned around he saw Tyrone standing on the bank above his shoes, ready to douse them with what remained in his bucket.

"My watch!" Galen screamed.

Tyrone reached into Galen's shoe and found a silver Timex with a plain black band, set ten minutes fast. He grinned. "I'mana take you watch and drown it."

"You better not or you're gonna be drownded!" Galen shouted pathetically. He stood on the edge of the creek with a bucket, ready to retaliate on one of Tyrone's sandals.

"I'mana count to five and you gonna find my other shoe," Tyrone ordered. "One! Two! Three! Four . . . !"

Galen emptied the bucket on Tyrone's sandal.

"I don't care, it's already wet!" Tyrone sneered, then he winked at Franklin. "I ain't gonna hurt his watch," he confided. He wiped some mud from his head and pretended to rub it on the face of the dial. Galen watched, shivering with humiliation, his lower lip jutting out, leaves clinging to his wet hair.

"It's slowin' down! It's slowin' down!"

"You better not!"

"It done stop already." Tyrone held the watch to his ear and shook his head sadly. Galen sat on the upturned bucket and started to cry.

"He jokin', Galen!" Franklin shouted.

"He's *always* jokin'."

Tyrone returned the watch to Galen's shoe and walked up the creek a bit to launder his shirt and socks.

"Hey, Galen!" Franklin shouted consolingly. "Don't Tyrone's eyes look like he's goin' asleep?"

Galen smirked through his tears.

"Hey, Tyrone!" Franklin continued. "You tired? Galen say you look like you fallin' asleep."

"Suck an egg."

"Galen say your head look like an egg."

Galen began to pee on Tyrone's sandal.

Tyrone didn't look up. He wrung out his socks and hung them over a limb. He is used to hearing gibes about his appearance. He leaned over into the creek and rinsed the mud from his stubbly hair.

"Tyrone, you know what?" Franklin laughed, as if Tyrone would appreciate this observation. "You look like a *clown*."

Tyrone crossed his arms and stared at Franklin. "Hey, Franklin, you look like a clown, too. Only one thing— you ain't got the big red nose. And in a minute I'mana give it to you."

"You look like you asleep! I wonder what you look like when you be sleepin'. Awake?"

"Suck an egg, chicken head."

"You ain't seen chicken head till you look in a mirror."

"What you see in the mirror is rat face."

"Yeah, I seen rat face in the mirror already. It was you tryin' to be me. You tryin' to get my handsomeness."

Through the woods they heard Quill Peachey calling them to chores.

"Uh-oh. Now we gonna get it!" Franklin stood and dusted his rump. His clothes were perfectly dry. He picked up the shovel and a bucket and walked with Luke and Galen back up the cow path. Tyrone sat on a rock and listened to them leave. Franklin had them singing as they walked up the hill: *"Are you sleeping, are you sleeping, Brother Tyrone? Brother Tyrone?"*

"You don't know his real name yet," said Galen. "It's Trouble. That's what they call him in Queens."

Franklin laughed. *"Your head is like a cracked egg, your head is like a cracked egg, Brother Trouble. Brother Trouble."*

D.J. Jackson's plate was already piled high with corncobs and chicken bones as he brushed the flies from his macaroni salad and took another piece of chicken from the grill. The new pencil behind his ear read: DO UNTO OTHERS AS YOU WOULD HAVE THEM DO UNTO YOU: THE GOLDEN RULE. It was just getting dark, and already the skyrockets were fulminating on the horizon, over the heads of Presbyterians gathered to celebrate Independence Day.

Norm laughed. "Hey, boy! You're getting a little gut on you! You're always talking about me!"

D.J. looked at the burgeoning paunch that had pushed his belt to the last notch. In a week's time he had gone from a size 12 to a 14, and had to borrow a pair of Drill's slacks to wear to church. He reached over and poked

Norm's belly. "Yeah, let's talk about you."

Norm opened his hands to the picnic spread: applesauce, zucchini bread, potato chips, and a tub of homemade ice cream. "Country cooking. How do you like the chicken?"

"I *love* this part of the chicken, whatever it is." D.J. sunk his teeth deep into the flesh.

"The breast," said Martha.

Drill snickered.

"Yeah. The breast," D.J. mumbled. He set the breast aside uneaten and resumed chewing his gum, which had been stored during the meal behind a molar.

"Bet you don't eat like this in New York!" Drill said before Martha hushed him. Drill was in a competitve mood. "Eatin' all them *hog jaws* and *guts* and stuff like that!"

"I bet you ain't never had no egg foo yung, neither," D.J. replied coolly. "You come to New York sometime and my mother make it for you."

"We had Chinese food one time," Martha said quickly. "That time we went to escort and got lost in Chinatown. Remember, Norm?"

"Um." Norm was watching the fireworks in the darkening sky. The Fourth of July with its mock bombardments is an uncomfortable holiday for him. It reminds him that Mennonites did not fight for American independence and never defended it when the flashings on the horizon were real wars. Instead, they served as conscientious objectors. Norm and Martha had changed bedpans in a Cincinnati mental hospital during the first two years of their marriage. Nonetheless, war never changed their lives the way it did for some people in the valley. Today when Norm was cutting alfalfa in his high field he could see the Presbyterian cemetery on the next hillock and the tiny American flags on the graves of the veterans.

"Another thing," said Drill. "I wish he wouldn't wear that stupid ol' pencil to church. It embarrasses me. *Everybody* talks about it." Drill innocently pursed his lips, which were gory with barbecue sauce. "I bet his mother doesn't let him wear it when he goes to church in New York."

"I ain't go to church in New York," said D.J., although that fact is commonly known around the Kanagy table. "Sunday mornin' I be sellin' the *Daily News.* Gotta earn a livin' sometime."

"Earn a living!" Drill jeered. "And go spend it all on comic books and roller-skating!"

"'Cept when football season rolls around . . ." D.J. paused to let the mention of football penetrate Drill's envious attention. "Ain't no time to be skatin' when I be *in training.*"

Drill made a sour face. The sport of football is discouraged in the Belleville Mennonite School, which Drill attends. Most parents believe the game is too violent; they prefer soccer. Norm won't let his son play, or even watch football on television at a friend's house. Despite this, Drill is an avid and knowledgeable fan. His favorite team is the Dallas Cowboys, and he owns a copy of Roger Staubach's autobiography, *First Down and Lifetime to Go,* which Norm tolerates because it is a Christian work.

"You play football on *Sundays?*" asked Martha.

"That's when we have our games, is Sunday mornin'. 'Course, we be practicin' all week." D.J. smiled at Drill. "I be playin' nearly every day."

"Oh, that's right," Martha remembered, "you're going to be a football player when you grow up."

"A football player or a artist," D.J. amended. "I know

I can be a artist, but you can't tell about football till I be older. If I be big enough, maybe I play."

"What position?" Drill had to ask.

"Wide receiver. 'Cause of my speed. Someday you prob'ly be seein' me play."

"I doubt Dad'll let me."

"Don't worry," Martha said generously, "if Darrell Christopher is playing we'll all go up. Maybe someday he'll be the wide receiver for the New York Jews."

*"Jets,"* D.J. sputtered incredulously. "The New York Jets!"

Norm laughed as he got up from the table. "Better go check the cows. Got two fresh tonight. You boys wanna come?"

"I guess so," said Drill. He and D.J. followed Norm into the lane, leaving the dishes on the table for Martha to clean up. Norm's mutt dog fell into step as they passed by.

Norm got a flashlight from the barn. The valley was black but there was still some light in the sky. They could see bats flitting overhead in the pasture. The fireworks thundered dully like a coming storm.

"Look here, she's fresh already." The beam of Norm's light found a new heifer calf on the ground being licked clean of afterbirth by her mother. The calf was already making motions to stand. Norm was relieved; in the last week he had had two calves born backward, both dead. A string of bad births can ruin a farmer.

"A free cow," D.J. marveled. "How many you got now?"

"I guess that makes fifty-six, and another one coming yet."

"Like, how much that cow cost if you buy him in a store?"

"When she's growed, a good milker will bring a thousand dollars, at least."

D.J. whistled. "So you made like two thousand dollars while you was eatin' dinner!"

"'Course, you don't like to sell the good ones, because they can earn you nearly that much a month in milk. Now, her mom gives me sixty pounds of milk a day."

D.J. examined the animal that generates more income every month than the Jackson family receives in welfare payments, and said in a low, appreciative voice, "Maybe I oughtta start learnin' how to be a farmer."

"It's not easy to get started. You need a lot of money."

"Like how much you need?"

"I guess the average farm around here might sell for a hundred thousand dollars. Then you'll spend forty thousand more for forty good cows and maybe sixty thousand for equipment. At least two hundred thousand just to get started."

"I guess that lets me out," D.J. said, laughing.

Norm found the other laboring cow lying in a dry rill near the fence. When the light hit her eyes, she stood up and swung her rear end angrily, as if she were trying to sling her creation out of her wretched body. Norm could see a pair of hooves poking out under her tail. The calf was coming out in the right direction but it was too early to know if it was alive. "I think we better get her in the barn," said Norm. "Go put some fresh straw in a stall and bring me a couple of clubs. You boys are gonna have to help me move her."

Drill ran down the lane to the barn.

The cow had settled on the rill as the spot to deliver, and she groaned a warning when Norm came closer. He retreated and leaned against the fence. She was making no progress. She flopped down and got up again; she walked in circles. Occasionally the hooves submerged inside her again entirely, then reappeared, no further birthed than before. A pair of protective bossies shuffled in front of her like nervous bodyguards.

"Last one she had got all fouled up," said Norm. "It was all turned around inside her. The vet came out and ran a wire down inside her and back out again, then he and I sawed the calf in half with that wire. Had to pull it out in pieces."

D.J.'s voice was dry. "Where'd you bury it at?"

"Ha. Well, you know you don't bury cows."

"You don't?"

"When you get a dead calf you usually send it off to the rendering plant. That's what they make dog food out of."

Drill came back carrying a broomstick and a two-by-four.

"Okay, I want you boys to man the gate. When I get her up to it, make sure she doesn't turn down the lane but goes straight into the barnyard."

"Do you think she'll charge you, Dad?"

"I don't know. She's sure acting nervous."

Norm took the two-by-four and walked wide around the cow. She revolved on her spot in the rill, keeping a nervous eye on Norm's progress. A series of pops and crackles from the fireworks made her shudder. Norm hummed soothingly.

"Be careful, Dad."

The cow had her head down. She thumped the earth with a front hoof.

Norm walked steadily toward her, humming and beating a rhythm in his hand with his club. The bodyguards backed off. The cow grunted and took a step to one side, then leaned forward again. Norm slapped his hand hard with the stick and kept humming, and kept coming. She danced aside as if she had suddenly come unstuck from the mud. Norm moved her out of the rill.

Once she was out of her spot, she gave him no trouble and passed without objection into the barnyard. Drill and D.J. shut the gate to the pasture and ran into the barn. Drill pushed a hay cart in the aisle past the vacant stall. The cow came bawling into the barn, and in a moment the calves in the other stalls were lowing in sympathy. Norm got her into the stall, then waved some green hay under her nose. She stuck her head through the bars to take a bite and Drill pulled a lever that shut the grid tight on her neck so she couldn't turn around.

"Whew," said Norm. He was wearing his sleeveless white tee shirt and the sweat was already soaking through. The barn was hot, and hoary with cobwebs. White miller moths circled the bare, white, dangling bulbs. D.J. sat on the steps to the hayloft with a pad in his lap and sketched the scene.

Norm squirted liquid soap on his right arm nearly to his shoulder. He stood behind the cow and reached into her, lubricating the opening with his soapy arm and feeling for the calf's head to make sure it wasn't entangled. His arm came out gleaming and streaky with blood. D.J. rolled his eyes.

Norm wrapped a length of twine around the protruding forelegs, then tied the other end to the two-by-four. He pulled hard and the cow made an enormous noise. The calf came all the way up to its muzzle, and D.J. could see its red tongue sticking out of the side of its mouth, like a cartoon character that has been knocked unconscious; then the calf disappeared, as if something inside were pulling it back in a tug-of-war. Norm heaved again and got no farther. He leaned back against the stall and shook little beads of sweat out of his hair. "You boys give me a hand," he panted.

D.J. applauded.

"Okay, smarty! Get yourself down here!"

The boys held one end of the two-by-four and Norm slipped the other end behind the small of his back, using the hind end of the cow to brace himself. On the count of three they all heaved, and the calf came gushing out on a tide of water and blood. It plopped softly into the fresh straw.

Norm tested the mother's milk.

The calf lay in a heap. D.J. guessed from all the blood that it must be dead. Then he saw that the calf was moving its head and stretching. "It a boy or a girl?" he asked.

"A big bull calf," said Norm. "What should we name him?"

"Firecracker," said D.J.

# Chapter 8

Macy, Rose, and Anna Louise sat on a worn gray comforter under the maple trees. Each girl had a black purse over her arm. "I'll be the teacher," said Anna Louise.

"Pretend you wouldn't like us to call you by your first name, and sometimes we make a mistake and you get awful mad and beat us like everything," Macy proposed.

Anna Louise handed out paper and pencils. "Everybody say good morning to the teacher."

"Good morning, Anna Louise!"

"Don't call me Anna Louise! Call me 'Miss Wilder.' "

"Who?"

"Wilder. Laura Ingalls Wilder. You know! She wrote *Little House on the Prairie.*"

"Then my name is Shirley," said Rose. "Shirley Wilder."

"My name is Farrah," said Macy. "Farrah Fawcett-Wilder."

"Now first, we're going to have geography. I want you'uns to write down as many countries as you can think of."

"Countries?"

"Like Greece," said Anna Louise. "But not in the United States. Like Greece. Or Switzerland. Just a whole mess like that."

"Can we say the states, Miss Wilder?" asked Macy.

"Uh-uh. Not states. Like Greece, and—"

"Italy," said Rose.

"Just wait, Shirley. Greece and Italy and all them that you studied in geography, but none in the United States. Okay. Ready—set—go."

Anna Louise went inside to fetch a box of pretzels and a pitcher of homemade root beer. In the background baby Timmy was crying and Ruth Byler was singing "I Want to Love Him More" as she cleaned house. Little Samuel came out to watch the girls play, then faced the side of the house and relieved himself.

"I can't spell Switzerland," Macy complained.

"Teacher, can we write the continents?" Rose hollered.

"Yes!" Anna Louise shouted from the kitchen. "Anything except the United States! Like Greece!"

"I didn't have geography this year," Rose muttered, "so it's no wonder I can't think of anything. I wish we were doing spelling."

"I don't study for spelling tests," Macy advised her. "I always get in the nineties."

"I got a hundred in all tests this year," said Rose. "The teacher said if we get a hundred six times we get a present. And I did and I got a *toothbrush*."

"Oh, my handwriting is horrible!"

"I know! I get terrible out of practice when I don't go to school. But like I was in Sam Detweiler's class and I was trying to write nice and neat and I always got Cs! Then I started to write big and kinda sloppy, and I got A-pluses and all whatnot."

The Amish school that Rose and Anna Louise attend resembles a public school in rural America at the turn of the century: a one-room affair, with a belfry, where the teaching philosophy is drilling the three Rs and the principal text is the *McGuffey's Reader*. Other subjects are English, which few Amish children can speak before they go to school, and High German, which enables them to read the German Bible. There are only eight grades in the Amish school; the ninth—and, for nearly all Amish children, the last—grade is a "vocational" class created to satisfy Pennsylvania compulsory attendance laws which require that a child remain in school until the age of fifteen. The vocational class meets on Wednesday nights and Saturdays and is devoted to discussions of homemaking and farming.

In the past, Amish children went to public school with everyone else in the valley, but the movement to consolidate public schools, along with the push to teach science that accompanied the American space effort, forced the Amish to construct their own schools. The result is that Rose and Anna Louise are more isolated from "English" society than their parents were.

The Amish school has very little in common with the urban public school of the sort that Macy Mizell attends, with its staff of certified teachers, doctors, counselors, and psychologists; its expensive modern teaching aids; its federally supported programs for children with learning disabilities and disadvantaged minorities; and especially its middle-class, technology-oriented system of values. As John Hostetler writes, "For the Amish, education is primarily social rather than individual. Its goal is not 'the freedom which exalts the individual' but social cohesion and social responsibility." Critical thinking is not so important as correct knowledge. As a result, the Amish school emphasizes drill and memorizing, rather than independent questioning. Hostetler compares the emphasis on group excellence, in which the entire class strives to do well, to the Soviet children's collectives.

In 1969, Professor Hostetler and Gertrude Enders Huntington studied achievement patterns in Amish schools. "Because of their limited access to mass media and because of the use of English as a second language, we anticipated incorrectly that the Amish would score lower than the non-Amish children in public school. We were surprised," the authors wrote in *Children in Amish Society: Socialization and Community Education.* Using standardized national measures such as the Iowa Test of Basic Skills and the Stanford Achievement Test, they found that "In spite of the limited exposure the Amish children have to radio, television, and modern school facilities and although the Amish teachers themselves have had only an eighth-grade education, the Amish pupils scored significantly higher in spelling, word usage, and arithmetic than the pupils in our sample of rural public schools. They scored slightly above the national norm in these subjects in spite of small libraries and limited equipment. The Amish pupils were equal to the non-Amish pupils in comprehension and in the use of reference material. They scored lowest in vocabulary. (No tests were given in German vocabulary.) In those aspects of learning stressed by the Amish culture, the Amish pupils out-performed pupils in the control group." Hostetler and Huntington attribute the success of the Amish schools to their careful integration into the Amish society. The schools are controlled by the parents; the teachers come from the community; the curriculum stresses skills that are obviously needed for living in the community.

The public school that Macy attends in Brooklyn is an immense, alien presence in her community. With its barred windows and security doors, it looks like an enemy fort. Inside, the lockers have been pried open and the walls are covered with graffiti. Despite the "professionalism" of the school, the staff is demoralized, and defensive about the low standards of achievement. With all the expertise and government money, the quality of the basic education Macy receives is no higher and possibly lower than its Amish counterpart.

Anna Louise returned with the snacks and placed them on a wooden table, then sat on the blanket and studied the bruises on her legs while the girls finished the test.

"Oooh, I can't think!" Macy whined.

"Okay, I'll give you a couple of hints. It can be in South America, but it can't be in the United States. It can be Bolivia."

"Can we do in the Bible, with the Holy Land?" asked Rose.

"Nope."

"Aaah! Not Judah or Samaria?"

"Mexico," said Anna Louise. "Now, that's the last hint I'm gonna give you."

Macy chewed on her pen and watched a parade of banties strut past.

"I have twelve," said Rose.

"Thirteen," said Macy.

"Okay, let me see. Shirley had Greece, Japan, China, Switzerland, Netherlands, Italy, Canada, Australia, Africa, Mexico, Greenland— Hey! That's not how you spell Chile!"

"It is so!"

"You spelled chilly, like you're cold. Not Chile like a country."

"She didn't know the difference!" said Macy, sadly amazed.

"Now let me read— What's your name again?"

"Farrah."

"Okay, Farrah. Let's see. Switzerland is misspelled; then Italy, Greece, Netherlands— What did you have here?"

"Oh no, no! I just have twelve, then."

"What did she have?" Rose insisted.

"I put Atlanta," Macy admitted.

"It's in Georgia!"

"I know. It's down south."

"Georgia's in the United States! She said *no states!*"

"It is not in the United States! It's in South America!"

"Honestly, Farrah! I'll have to get my United States map to prove it."

"First let's have the snacks," said Anna Louise. She poured the root beer into plastic glasses. Samuel tried to join them. "Okay," Anna Louise agreed, "but stay off the blanket. *Gey ab de deck.*"

Samuel continued to sit on a far corner of the blanket.

*"Gey ab!"* Macy thundered.

Samuel fled. Anna Louise was called to the telephone.

"You can't trust these bugs around here—they'll fly right in your mouth!" said Macy, hacking and spitting.

"I know, they're so filthy! Did you ever see a fly lay eggs? One day we cut off a round steak and I gave the bone to the dog, and I put it down on the porch and all these flies just swarmed right to it! And then in a minute we could see all these little white worms all over it. Just like that! Little white worms crawling all over this bone . . ."

"Yuchht!"

Anna Louise came rushing out. "Guess what? It's Barbara Zook's birthday and we're invited for cake and then her mom says we can have a slumber party in her playhouse!"

# Chapter 9

Ivan Stoltzfus was building a doghouse from leftover cedar planks, while Eddie Cato mimicked him by smashing ants with a hammer on the cement steps outside the workshop. David, the black terrier pup whose house was under construction, observed the executions from as far away from Eddie as his chain leash would reach.

In a moment Eddie yawned and walked over to hug the puppy, but the dog squirmed out of his arms and backed away whining, straining at the leash, in obvious terror. Eddie grabbed the leash and was whirling the puppy overhead like a toy airplane when Ivan came out with the completed house.

"Here, stop that!"

The puppy skidded on the gravel and lay pop-eyed and heaving. Eddie ran into the house to his sanctuary upstairs, where he could lock the door from the inside.

Ivan could not figure out Eddie's behavior. The boy seemed to love the dog, but he abused it mercilessly. And what should Ivan do about it? Eddie was plainly frightened of Ivan, just as the puppy was of Eddie, but he followed Ivan around most of the day, from a distance, watching what Ivan did and sometimes allowing himself to be drawn into shy conversation, his voice so quiet that Ivan had to strain to hear. Ivan had learned to keep an eye on him, because whenever Eddie was out of sight he was usually in trouble. One time he found Eddie leaning out of the loft window of the barn looking down at the ground—nearly a fifty-foot drop. Another time Ivan had almost run over Eddie with a tractor when Eddie jumped out from a tree in front of the forward wheels. As a rule, Ivan did not like to have boys on the farm because of their natural inclination to get into things that might hurt them: to play with the power tools, walk the rafters in the barn, toy with the livestock . . . but Eddie was worse than that, worse than reckless. He seemed headed almost deliberately for disaster.

Ivan and Aire had invited Fresh Air children every year of their marriage until last year, when they had decided that they were too old to worry about having New Yorkers underfoot. But shortly after the children arrived, Ann Peachey called and asked if they would take in a "special" child who had proved too much for a young couple to handle. His name was Eddie Cato, she said, a little "Porta Rickan" from the Bronx, described by the medical sheet as being hyperactive and suffering from speech disabilities. If Ivan and Aire wouldn't take him in he would have to be returned to New York. This year, they thought a long time before inviting him back.

Eddie reappeared at the door of the workshop. Ivan pretended not to notice. He swept up the sawdust around the table saw and walked past Eddie to put the sweepings in the doghouse as a bed for the puppy. David was in his new home, hiding from his tormentor.

"Well, I guess we ought to make a sign for the pup," Ivan said. "You want to do that?"

Eddie nodded.

Ivan gave him a six-inch scrap of board and a felt-tip marker. Eddie wrote painstakingly in capital letters

DAVID. He insisted on nailing it up himself over the door of the house, while the terrier trembled inside. Ivan left him alone and headed for the barn. Eddie could see only the dark gleam of the pup's eyes. He reached in and David snapped at his hand.

"I goin' kill! Kill-kill-kill—!" Eddie struck the doghouse with the hammer as hard as he could, breaking a hole in the roof. The dog yelped and Ivan came running out of the barn. Eddie gave him a quick, cold look and flung the hammer at his head. Then he turned and ran toward the house.

Ivan was stunned by the slap of the hammer, which had glanced off his temple. He felt his wound in puzzlement, and then, his face turning nearly as red as the blood dripping into his beard, he chased after Eddie with the hammer in his hand.

Eddie is a product of the Bureau of Child Welfare, which took him into its custody immediately after his birth. His mother, who named him, surrendered him at the hospital. She told her friends that he was born dead.

Instead, he was born a junkie, a legacy from his mother, who passed her addiction through her bloodstream. Eddie spent the first week of his life in a detoxification program. When he got out of the hospital he was placed with a foster mother.

The woman was a "professional," meaning that she kept enough children in her house to live off the income the state provided. She operated her business as efficiently as any chicken farmer in the valley, and with a similar degree of remorselessness. Eddie lived for eighteen months in a playpen, with no maternal affection. When he got rambunctious and tried to escape from his pen, his "mother" would strap him down. He was finally rescued by a case worker, but by then he was "almost catatonic."

Eddie was placed with Rose Mbonzo, a hybrid rose of the sort that grows only in New York: a Puerto Rican orphan, Jehovah's Witness, widow of an African soccer player, and foster mother to three children—two teen-aged black girls and Eddie. She is a round-faced, smiling woman with dark eyes as flickering and bright as a jack-o'-lantern's. Her hair is drawn up in a gray-black bun atop her head, counterpoised by looping gold earrings. She has slender limbs but a corpulent midsection, and the elastic-band slacks she prefers to wear expand around her waist in a wide dish so that she resembles a two-legged birdbath. When Rose laughs she puts one hand on her belly and waves the other in the air in an "Aw, g'wan!" gesture. Her laugh is like an avalanche rumbling out of her cavernous interior, making the room quake.

Rose and her children live on Avenue St. John in the South Bronx, formerly a fashionable street now devastated by arson and vandalism, where the burned-out windows face each other from either side of the street like rows of skulls on an anthropologist's shelves. Only two of the grand old stone apartment houses on the block are still inhabited. In the summer one can stand in the middle of the avenue (the traffic problem left with the population) and spot Rose Mbonzo's apartment by the box of petunias outside her window—an unexpected refinement.

In many ways Rose Mbonzo is like an Amishwoman of the Kishacoquillas Valley. She bakes her own bread and pastries, and boils the clothes clean on the kitchen stove. In the winter she saves electricity by burying her frozen foods in the snow on the fire escape. As a Jehovah's Witness she believes in non-violence, an attitude that takes on an almost hopeless poignancy in the South Bronx, where violence pervades the atmosphere as thoroughly as the stink of incinerators and automobile exhaust. From her window Rose can watch children vandalizing the empty buildings, or teenagers stripping a stolen car—in broad daylight, with no fear of being reported. When Rose goes out and leaves the children in the apartment she often fears that someone will break in and kill them. For no reason.

Rose campaigns against the violence in her children. "It's a little like living in a prison," she says; "everyone is so tense, people on edge all the time. There is a lot of violence in the way we raise our children, a lot of violence in our voices. You see mothers get angry and slap their children—what does that teach them?

"In the summer everyone is all heated. I don't want my children on the streets. You have to take time with them, give them something to do. We have music lessons, and I try to get them to read. I used to have a TV in every room. But it was just too much electricity. And you see children picking up attitudes. They get sophisticated; they know too much. The TV is used to pacify the children, but it pacifies them with violence.

"So I got rid of all the TVs. At first I thought the children wouldn't be able to function, but as soon as I took them away, the children started reading and using the encyclopedias. I always emphasize reading. I don't have no fancy furniture, but I'll tell you one thing: we got books."

Rose was a keypunch operator and studying to be a computer programmer, but she had to give up her studies when Eddie Cato came to her; and after a while, she gave up her job, too. For the first six months Eddie lay in the crib making water movements as if he were still in the womb, as if at two years of age he were going to start all over again. He showed no affection for anyone. When he learned to walk, he would go straight for the door. "He used to run out," Rose recalls. "I couldn't leave him with a baby-sitter because it was dangerous. He couldn't mix with other children; he would beat the smaller ones. Sometimes I would be on a bus and he would throw a tantrum and we'd have to get off the bus, no matter where we were. Once I had a dog, a Labrador retriever, and when Eddie was four he bit the dog's ear so severely that the vet had to take it off.

"I took him to the doctor and he gave me medicine for his behavior, for his hyperactivity. I gave him a dose and watched him, and he was like a drunk, eyes glazed, making foolish movements. I couldn't give it to him anymore. So instead I had to stay up at night, 'cause he got it all confused. Day was night and night was day. I used to be in the street with him at three or four in the morning and he was full of activity. But I had decided he didn't need a system full of medication."

Rose believes she is fighting for Eddie's soul. To reach him she has to take risks. One of the risks is sending him to public school, where there is always a danger that he will do something terrible, or provoke one of the older children into hurting him. Another risk is sending him away through the Fresh Air Fund in the summer. All the time he was in the country last year, Rose was terrified of the phone ringing with some awful news (she understood what he was capable of doing); but she didn't call him herself, didn't even write because she didn't know what effect a letter from home might have. It is important for Eddie to be away from her, she thinks; he gets too used to her, and even if he is not "close" in the way most sons are to their mothers, he is even more dependent.

She fears what might happen to Eddie's small sense of identity if he is ever taken away from her. After all, he is not adopted (the welfare office turned down her request), so his future is uncertain. Better for him to have a taste of separation in the country, where he can wear himself out in a way he never could in the city—run and run and run and exhaust the anger and frustration.

When Eddie came home last year he had a crooked smile that Rose couldn't read and two missing teeth. He brought the teeth home in a plastic coin purse (believing, in his version of the tooth-fairy myth, that if you lost a tooth you would have to pay to get a new one). He didn't say anything at first. Rose had learned that Eddie gets annoyed if you try to pump him for information. So she acted nonchalant and asked what he would like to do, read a book or go for a Coke or what. He wanted to go outside. Downstairs in the doorway men sat in their undershirts drinking beer and playing dominoes and filling the air with the crackling, electric sounds of Spanish. The avenue was lined with junked cars, some long abandoned, tags expired, listing to one side. Rose and Eddie walked to the corner, where there is a spindly maple, not much taller than a full-grown man, its leaves yellowed by city toxins. Eddie began to climb it. The tree swayed under him, it could barely sustain his weight (although he weighed only as much as a medium-sized dog), but Eddie got into it nonetheless and sat there hugging its slender trunk as if he were in the highest branches of a forest giant, with the breeze in his face, on top of the world.

Ivan Stoltzfus pursued Eddie into the house, not sure yet what he was going to do when he caught him. Ivan's head throbbed. Eddie knocked over a chair and hit the stairs, pulling on the railing as if it were a life rope. Ivan stumbled behind, reaching the top of the stairs just as Eddie slammed the door, but Ivan didn't stop and before Eddie got the lock in place Ivan crashed in.

Ivan has raised five children. He is secure in what he knows about bringing up children, especially boys. They need a firm hand. Spare the rod and spoil the child, a belief prescribed by the Bible and confirmed many times in Ivan's own household. Ivan likes to quote a parable he read in a Sunday School lesson: A woman entered a shepherd's hut at night. Inside, she saw a shape move in the shadow outside the lamplight. "What is that creature?" she asked the shepherd. "It is a lamb," he said. "I broke its leg. He was leading the other sheep astray. The first day he took no food, and the second day he took no food either, but the third day he took and licked my hand."

"Punishment is like that," says Ivan. "People sometimes hate to do it, but it is often rewarding afterwards. But we daresn't do it out of anger!"

Ivan closed the door and sat on the bed. Eddie was whimpering in the corner.

"You did a bad thing, Eddie," Ivan said. "When we are mad we should not hurt others in our anger. I'm going to spank you now, but I'm not going to do it in anger. There's a difference between you throwing this hammer at me and me spanking you. What you did you did out of anger and hate. What I do I do out of love."

Ivan seized the shivering child and carried him outside. He cut a switch from the willow tree beside the pond, just as he had many times in the past with his own children, and as his father had done when he was young. Eddie waited helplessly. When Ivan had shaved the switch he pulled Eddie's pants down and whipped him hard, leaving red welts on his skinny buttocks. Then he buttoned Eddie's pants and left him to cry it out.

An hour later Eddie came into the workshop and hugged Ivan's leg. "I didn't mean to kill you, Dad," he said.

Eddie played quietly. Aire was inside canning cherries. Ivan took the tractor out and worked in the fields. He resolved that he would take Eddie fishing in the creek sometime, and perhaps make him a toy in the workshop to take home, as he often made games and doll furniture for his grandchildren.

When Ivan drove back to the barn, the first thing he noticed was Eddie walking across the drive with the switch in his hand, going into the house. Aire was weeding the garden. The chain leash holding the puppy was missing and the dog was not in sight.

"Where is David?" he called to Eddie, but he couldn't quite make out Eddie's response, something about ". . . on the sewing machine."

Ivan wasn't sure what Eddie said, but when he parked the tractor he could hear the puppy yelp, and hear, as he ran into the house, the switch whistling and Eddie explaining, "I not angry. I not angry."

# Chapter 10

Macy, Rose, and Anna Louise traveled the half-mile to Barbara Zook's house on roller skates and bicycles, trailed by their younger brothers, who went for cake.

Henry Zook's farm is an attractive piece of land, divided by a slender stream which shines like mercury in the glow of early evening. Beside the road there is a steep brick farmhouse, with an expandable gate to contain the babies at the top of the steps. Below the house is Henry's barn and milking parlor (he does not use electric milkers), and behind the barn is a two-story chicken house which looks like a small army barracks.

The birthday girl was snaring pullets when the guests arrived. Macy, Rose, and Anna Louise found her padding barefoot through the mat of feathers that covered the floor of the chicken house like a heavy snow. The hens cleared a swath in the range of her crooked stick, crowding into the corners and leaping onto the rafters. The room stank of ammonia. When Barbara spotted a hen she wanted she would thrust her stick into the mob and yank out her mark by its wrinkled yellow leg. The hens came out squawking furiously, flapping clouds of down into the hot air. Some of the feathers settled into the girls' braids or clung to their perspiring foreheads. Anna Louise and Rose helped Barbara carry four hens outside.

Macy balked when she saw Barbara's father standing under an apple tree behind the Zook house with an ax over his shoulder. Barbara chided her. "Why, we have to kill them *sometime*. Besides, these'uns are going crippled. They're growing too fast for their legs. If we didn't slaughter them the other chickens would be after them. You can see already—" She started to point out a sore on the neck of one of the hens but Macy turned away. She went off and stood by herself behind the picket fence that surrounds the apple orchard.

Redheaded Henry Zook stood in a ring of interested children. He placed the neck of the first hen on the chopping block between two ten-penny nails, and gripped the nervous yellow legs with his other hand. The chicken lay helpless, one round eye staring directly at the sky. Henry sliced the head off neatly, and it fell among the rotting green apples in the grass. Macy heard the whomp and peeked through her fingers, watching in horrified amazement as the headless animal chased the squealing children around the apple trees.

Mrs. Zook hurried from the kitchen carrying a galvanized tub of steaming water. She soaked the hens in the scalding water, which turned muddy with blood. In a moment, she sat the corpses on a newspaper for plucking.

"Oooh, I hate the smell when you kill chickens," Anna Louise sniffed. It was a thick, mustardy odor which mingled with the sour fragrance of the bad apples. The girls helped pull out the feathers, which came out easily, like grass from wet sod. Mrs. Zook set the plucked carcasses in a row with their yellow legs stuck into the air.

The girls found Macy riding her bike in the road, pedaling fast with no hands. "Got any more surprises?" She was angry.

"How'd you like the slaughter?" Anna Louise laughed. "Bet you never saw anything like that before!"

"I can't *stand* the sight of blood!"

"What about your own blood?"

Macy circled and zoomed past the girls again. Her face was grim and firmly set. "It's a sin to kill chickens!" she hollered over her shoulder. She pedaled over a hill and out of sight.

The children were sitting on the porch eating birthday cake when she returned and blithely parked her bike beside the picket fence. "Will you ever eat chicken again, Macy?" they taunted.

"No!"

Macy took a very large slice of cake and sat morosely on the bottom step with her back to the chorus.

"Won't you eat it off the grill, yet?" Barbara Zook asked.

Macy ruminated over a bite of white-frosted spice cake. "Yeah, I guess so," she mumbled, and took another bite.

After the cake, the children followed Macy to the door of the milking parlor, which was vacant except for a single sick cow they could see who stood in her stall and eyed the children nervously. Barbara explained that the cow had "scars"—like ulcers—and she was on a special diet to regain her equilibrium. Macy edged into the parlor on Elmer Byler's ten-speed bike. Anna Louise and Rose came scraping behind on roller skates, followed by Barbara Zook and her sister Sylvia on bicycles (Sylvia's had training wheels), then by Samuel Byler pulling his brother Myron in a yellow Western Flyer wagon, the younger Zook children on tricycles with rubber horns, and finally several of their blond cousins, who circled the nauseated cow behind the mechanized caravan—which gained in noise as it increased in speed.

The Byler girls catapulted each other on skates, bicycles whizzed, white knees pumped in frenzy, the Western Flyer made a long yellow smear around the room, and the groans of the cow were lost in the clamor.

Suddenly the children left, launched through the door like a rock from a sling and leaving the cow in the echoing aftermath, rolling her head around and around in a dizzy orbit of the state of equilibrium.

"There was an Amishman and an Englishman and they were up in the barn fixing the roof," said Rose, "and there was this big pile of manure just below them. And then the Amishman jumped down. And the Englishman called down, 'How deep is that manure?' And the Amishman said, 'Ankle deep!' So the Englishman jumped down. It went way up to his shoulders, and he said, 'I thought you said it was ankle deep!' And the Amishman said, 'It *is* ankle deep—if you go in head first!'"

The girls were in the playhouse, which is a disused larder that Barbara had furnished with carpet scraps and an end table. On the wall there was a paint-by-the-numbers landscape accomplished by Sylvia Zook: a scarlet barn beside an aquamarine creek. The pantry shelves were lined with blue paper and exhibited Christmas cards and birthday greetings from past years. The remainder of the shelf space was stacked with dessert plates, saucers, cups, and glasses. Anna Louise admired the room, which Barbara had "red up" for the slumber party. "She's going to be a particular housewife!"

Macy lay with her head in Barbara's lap while Barbara stroked her hair. "You sure got a lot of old dishes!" Macy observed.

"Mom got them down from the attic. We used to have church in our house when we were Amish. After church we had to feed great numbers of people. They used to call our church 'bean-soupers' because we always served bean soup!"

"You were buggy Amish?" Macy gasped.

"They were yellow-toppers," Anna Louise explained. "Can you imagine Barb and Sylvia in those black aprons?"

"You mean you can change religions up here?"

"Of course!" said Barbara. "Can't you in New York?"

"What are you now, then?"

"They're Holdemans," said Anna Louise.

"We're not Holdemans, we're Conservative Mennonites. Holdemans is just a name they gave us after the person who founded the church. We're really Church of God in Jesus Christ Mennonites."

"We call them Holdemans," Anna Louise said firmly.

Barbara lit a candle on the table and the girls changed into their nightgowns, which were long cotton prints except for Macy's—a "shorty" type in flaming-red acrylic. They sat in a circle and drank strawberry punch. Anna Louise, who strived to look older than eleven, had pinned up her hair and looked comparatively matronly despite the scabs on her elbows and the skate key on her wrist. She took a sip of the punch. "Oooh, this is terrible," she sighed. Macy looked surprised. "Terrible *good,*" Anna Louise giggled.

"There were twelve boys and they were gonna pick apples," said Barbara. "Each picked one. How many apples did each pick? I mean, how many apples did the twelve boys pick?"

"Twelve?"

"One!" said Barbara. "Each picked one."

"You said how many did the twelve boys pick, so they would've picked twelve!" Rose contended.

"Well, *each* picked one . . ."

"No, if they *all* picked one, that'd be one," said Anna Louise. "They *each* picked one, that'd be twelve."

Macy and Rose agreed.

"No!" Barbara shouted. "Each! Each was the boy's name. *Each* picked one. How many apples did they pick? None of the other boys picked apples, just Each."

"Oh."

"I got one Rose told me," said Macy.

"Let me tell it!"

Macy ignored her. "There was this smart boy, right? It was a smart boy and a dumb boy, and this dumb boy's mother—"

"The *smart* boy's mother!"

"The *smart* boy's mother invited the dumb boy's mother to go shopping."

"No! His mother—"

"*Anyway,* the smart boy says, 'Let's play store and you be the clerk. So, what you sellin', dude?' And he goes, 'I don't know.' Smart boy says, 'Don't say that, say *shoestrings.* Now how much are they?' 'I don't know.' 'You ain't s'posed to say that! You s'posed to say two for a nickel! Right? So, are they any good?' 'I don't know.' 'Don't say that! Say some are, some aren't.' 'Okay.' The smart boy says, 'What you sellin'?' The dumb boy goes, 'Shoestrings.' He says, 'How much are they?' 'Two for a nickel.' 'They any good?' 'Some are, some aren't.' And the smart boy says, 'I don't think I'll buy any.' So the dumb boy says, uh . . ."

" 'I don't care!' "

"And the dumb boy says, 'You ain't s'posed to say—' "

"*Smart* boy!"

"And the smart boy says, 'You ain't s'posed to say that! Say if you don't, somebody else will!' So the smart boy says again, 'What you sellin'?' He says, 'Shoestrings.' The smart boy says, 'How much are they?' Dumb boy goes, 'Two for a nickel.' The smart boy says—hold it—smart boy says . . .''

" *'Are they any good'!* " Rose screamed, exasperated.

"And the dumb boy goes, 'Some are, some aren't.' The smart boy says, 'I don't think I'll buy any.' The dumb boy says, 'If you don't, somebody else will.' All right. A stranger comes to town.''

"One day, this dumb boy met a stranger," said Rose.

"Right. The stranger says, 'What's the name of this town?' The dumb boy says, 'Shoestrings.' He says, 'What's the population?' He goes, 'Two for a nickel.' 'Are all the people as dumb as you?' 'Some are, some aren't.' He says, 'You wanna punch in the nose, dude?' 'If you don't, somebody else will.' "

Macy finished the joke lamely and stared into the hub of the silent circle, where the outstretched legs met like spokes.

Barbara disappeared with the flashlight and returned with the remainder of the birthday cake. They relit the candles and sang "Happy Birthday":

> *"Happy Birthday to you!*
> *You belong in a zoo!*
> *You look like a monkey*
> *And you act like one too!"*

Barbara blew out thirteen candles. Although by valley standards she is a big girl for her age, Macy is already larger and more developed at the age of eleven.

"Thirteen!" Anna Louise exclaimed. "And tomorrow I'll be twelve."

"That's right, one day apart. A year and a day."

"I heard already that twelve is the worst year of your life."

"It *was!*" Barbara covered her head with a pillow to shut out the awful memory.

"That makes you both Cancers," said Macy.

"Oh, really?"

"You mean you don't know your horoscopes?" Macy stared in astonishment, as if they had just said that the earth is flat. "In New York, *everybody* knows their sign. Like my science teacher, she talks a lot about astrology. She has class parties when the signs change."

"See, we don't study science," Anna Louise explained.

"You know, I never known no one who died on their birthday," Macy realized. "But I do know somebody that got divorced on her birthday."

"I guess most people in New York are divorced," said Rose.

Macy nodded.

"Well, there's not many people that do that here. Not that *we* know."

"You barely hear of anybody getting divorced," Anna Louise agreed. "I never heard of anybody in the valley."

"I think John Wilson's mom is," said Barbara.

"Is she!"

"I'm not *sure,* but I think so."

"She's Presbyterian."

"When I grow up, I may not want to be married anyway," said Rose. "What I'd like to do is live in a trailer and have an orchard and go to the Sale Barn every Wednesday. That's something you can't do if you're married. My mom never gets caught up with the patching."

"Not be married!" Barbara was shocked.

"I'd like to be a nurse or a housewife," said Anna Louise. "If I was to be a nurse I'd like to go around and deliver food to people."

"When I grow up," said Macy, "I just wanna be smaller."

"You're just lucky you're not small!" said Anna Louise, who is.

"Yes. Think about Irene Peight! She's gotta go to school next year!"

"They say she's smart."

"Poor thing, when she goes to school. Everybody will be carrying her around and everything. Her mom don't like her to go in public. People used to come in by busloads to see that child. And she was so *disgusted*— Irene's mom. They would say they were just in the neighborhood and wanted to stop in and see her. And in church, mothers would let their two-year-olds carry her around as if she were a toy."

"One time she was playing hide-and-go-seek and she crawled in her dad's boot and went to sleep. They couldn't find her for hours!"

"I saw a little lady at the Sale Barn—"

"Aaah! A wee thing!" Anna Louise interrupted. "As little as me!"

"—and she was pretty old. Her head was big like a woman and she was like a woman down to here. And then her legs, oooh! They were so short! Oh, she was terrible little! She was in a stroller, like."

"It was a cart, like."

"I think she must have been pretty old."

"In the circus they got midgets," said Macy. "They got ladies with beards—"

"Were you ever in a *circus?*" Rose gasped.

"Weren't you?"

"Uh-uh. We never even *hear* of any."

"I never been either," Macy confessed. "I never could say that name anyway."

"What name?"

"Ringling Brothers, Barnum Ba—" She laughed. "I never could say that."

"What are you trying to say?"

"I just have to think about it for a while."

"Think about *what?*"

"Ringling Brothers, Barnum Bailey Circus."

The girls mouthed the words. "Ringling Brothers Baby Circus," said Barbara.

"Barnum Bailey!" Macy screamed. "You said *Baby!*"

"Some people can't say Kishacoquillas," Barbara said pointedly.

"Kishacowho?"

"Kilafish ilafi colafo quillafill lalafas."

"What's *that?*"

"Kishacoquillas in pig latin."

"I ain't never heard pig latin like that."

"Macy knows a song in Dutch!" Anna Louise announced.

"I ain't singin' it," Macy stated emphatically, appreciating the pleas that followed.

"Macy, I'll help you. Honestly!"

"Okay. Let me put my pretzels down and take another drink." Macy readied herself slowly. The tune was "Frère Jacques":

> *"Schwatza Suzy, schwatza Suzy,*
> *Vie bisch tu? Vie bisch tu?*
> *Habbe quill a dange,*
> *Habbe quill a dange,*
> *Vie bisch tu? Vie bisch tu?*
>
> *Black-eyed Susan, black-eyed Susan*
> *How are you? How are you?*
> *Very well, I thank you,*
> *Very well, I thank you,*
> *How are you? How are you?"*

Macy followed the song with several cartwheels from her cheerleading routine.

Barbara decided it was time to go to bed. "I hope we haven't got any nightwalkers in here," she said as she blew out the candle.

"One time there was this boy named Elmer's Steve," Rose whispered, "and his parents were away so these other parents were there, named Dan and Heddie, and they had this baby in the crib and they were laying in bed and it was night, I guess, and they saw this person that came up to them and looked in the crib for a long time—"

"He was just having a nightmare," Anna Louise explained.

"Who?"

"Elmer's Steve."

"He just went over and looked in the crib, stood there for a while, then he went and held Dan's clothes up!"

The dark room erupted in naughty giggles.

"He said it scared them most out of their wits. Boy, I'm glad we don't have no nightwalkers in our room!"

"One time I dreamed about TV," said Macy. "I used to always look at it. I'd do *anything* to look at it. So one day I dreamed my stepfather said, 'You'll do anything for me, just to look at it.' And I said, 'Yeah! Anything! Anything!' He said, 'All right, pee on the floor!' In my clothes and all. And I just—*psssst!*"

"Oh, *Macy!*"

"I'm just crazy 'bout lookin' at TV."

"Where's the flashlight?" asked Anna Louise. "I guess we ought to visit Miss Fanny."

Outside, the noise of the cicadas had found a pulse. The girls filed into the dark behind the beam of the flashlight. It was a cool and starlit night, with a crescent moon. Macy never sees the stars in New York; in fact, she seldom looks up. A breeze came over the rise, bringing a moist chill off the pasture. Macy and Rose shivered as they sat on Miss Fanny, a two-seater outhouse situated in the grape arbor. Barbara asked what time it was.

"Ten after twelve."

"Happy birthday, Anna Louise."

# Chapter 11

That night Macy had a dream, a variation of a dream she often has. She is in her living room in New York and it is full of men, "like devils"—red-faced, that is, like hot coals—standing around a fire in the middle of the floor, laughing and casting huge shadows on the walls behind them. There is a man's body on the sofa. His face is familiar to Macy: a handsome, goateed man with a slender face and long fingers crossed on his chest.

Suddenly the devils stop their celebration. They sense that somebody is watching them. Macy! She is terrified that they will find her and throw her out the window. She dreams of shaking her mother, whose bed is only a few feet away. Wake up, wake up! I'm having a bad dream! Somebody in the living room, a body on the sofa! Her mother rises and turns on the light in the living room. Ain't nobody here, Macy, see for yourself. Macy sees shadows moving and hears scuffling behind the couch. She knows when her mother goes back to bed the devils will come out again.

Macy's mother, Jolene Thomas, doesn't like to hear about her daughter's dreams. She has enough to worry about. Jolene is a computer programmer in a Manhattan hospital, working from 3:00 P.M. until eleven at night and often into the early morning. She is usually asleep when Macy leaves for school and gone when Macy comes home. Jolene's boyfriend, Carlos Diaz, the father of Macy's half-sister, works the swing shift in a foundry, and his hours change every ten days. Macy seldom knows whom she is going to eat with, breakfast or dinner. If not Jolene or Carlos, it may be her grandmother, or one of Carlos's sisters.

Amid the disorder, Macy sleeps and dreams. She wakes up hard in the mornings, and never feels rested. In the summer, when there's "no reason" to get up, Macy sleeps half the day, going to bed around ten at night and rising twelve or thirteen hours later.

Anna Louise and Rose Byler are amazed at Macy's reputation as a slugabed, for although she is not an enthusiastic riser in Big Valley, she is always up before eight to gather eggs and to help with the chores. They repeat the stories that Macy tells on herself. "One time in New York Macy went to bed and way early in the morning she woke up and asked her mom what time it was, and then she said good night and went right back to sleep and slept till three o'clock!" says Anna Louise. "I was sleepy!" Macy explains. "I went to bed at eleven and woke up at nine, and I was cryin'. So I went back to sleep. Not exactly till three o'clock! About two-thirty—sump'm like that."

As it happens, Macy's bedroom is open to her mother's, and her mother's bed—shared by Carlos—is only four steps from Macy's. Even whispers pass across the space. Jolene and Carlos used to be more careful in what they did or said, but after a while they forgot about Macy. She is always asleep when Jolene gets home, and when Macy sleeps she is dead to the world, or seems to be.

Macy keeps a guarded distance from her mother's

lover. On the evenings when he doesn't work and is home with Macy and his own child, she behaves as if he is actually absent. Carlos is soft-spoken and tries to be kind, but he cannot win Macy over. He never tells her what to do, and after the first several years he gave up trying to make easy conversation. Macy's eyes turn cold whenever he feels like talking.

She often imagines how her life would be if her father were alive. She thinks of him as being firm, like Daniel Byler, and with Daniel's gentle sense of humor. If her father were alive, perhaps her family would sit around a big dining table, instead of individually at odd hours at the kitchen counter. They would have time together. Jolene would work a job with regular hours, or just stay at home, like Ruth Byler, keeping house and raising children. Life would be filled with reliable routines, with good-night prayers, with certain discipline.

Macy's summer vacations in Big Valley have become another life for her, and she nourishes that life through the year with devoted correspondence. Macy is alternately exhilarated and depressed after reading the letters from Pennsylvania, so that Jolene has begun to dread seeing them in the mail. If the letter is from Anna Louise it is usually an affectionate but perfunctory note. "I just want to write you a short little letter to tell you to send me a picture of you and Chamall [Macy's half sister]. So when I get city-sister sick I can look at it and think of the time when you will come back to the country. I will send you another picture of me and Rose. Return it when you come." Rose is the more passionate correspondent. "It's starting to warm up a little now," she wrote in March. "Am I ever glad! Are you glad to come to the country again? to the flies and the bees? sweet corn and parties? *I hope!* I MISS YOU!"

In the past year Macy has begun to think of moving to the Kishacoquillas Valley when she grows up. For her, it is a perfectly acceptable idea that she should want to leave the place where she lives, even though that may involve leaving her family and friends. It is the same impulse that made Jolene flee the rural South, and Carlos leave Venezuela. With their combined incomes the family is off welfare and upwardly mobile—and physically mobile as well. In the past four years they have gotten out of three different neighborhoods. They are immigrants from the ghetto, and although the apartment they have on Flatbush Avenue is cramped and hardly luxurious, it is comfortably furnished with shag carpets, a color television set, and even a swank bar for weekend entertaining. They have accomplished all this with interminable hours of overtime, at the cost of being not so much a family as an economic alliance. When they get a little better off, they'll move somewhere else. Movement itself is mollifying. They do not have in mind a clear idea of where they are going, just of where they have come from.

Flatbush is not far enough for Macy. "I hate this—all this noise! And you know my best friend's boyfriend got killed. Some man shot him. Lots of boys get shot. It's so dangerous and awful here. You can't ride bike—if you want to ride bike on these streets people think you're crazy and they might even hit you. In Big Valley you can ride bike and people just wave and say how ya doin'?"

Macy's life is prey to randomness: random noise, random attitudes, random violence, and in a way, a random family. At any moment circumstances may change dramatically. Someone may leave. Someone may die. When Macy comes home she is always on her guard for signs that something has gone wrong. Burglars have broken in before, and Macy knows what to look for. Jolene talks about riding the subways by herself after midnight, and Macy wonders what would happen to her if her mother were raped and killed. Would Carlos take care of her? Whenever he spends the night somewhere else, Macy immediately suspects he will never come home again. If her father were alive, Macy believes, he would rescue her from her vague, dangerous, randomly frightening world.

Rose and Anna Louise sympathize with Macy's desire to leave the city, and yet moving to them is so momentous that they don't encourage her. Simply moving from one church to another, as Barbara Zook's family did, can bring censure from one's friends and one's own family. The Zooks are shunned by the Old Order Amish community, and although shunning does not pass on to unbaptized children, Barbara often feels its effect. There are places where she can go but her mother can't, people who will say hello to her but not to her parents. Barbara is often used to carry messages from Old Order relatives. To leave the valley altogether, as Daniel Byler dreams of moving to Alaska, means to abandon the "beloved community"—that carapace of thought and tradition that limits, defines, and protects a person's identity every moment of his life. Macy's spontaneous and anonymous existence in New York is replaced in Big Valley by a world so confiningly personal that virtually everything Rose and Anna Louise see or hear is a confirmation of their identity as Amish-Mennonite girls. For them, movement is so formidable that they will probably remain all of their lives in the same spot. But for Macy moving is easy, and she will inevitably move and move and move —further from the ghetto, perhaps, but not closer to the family and traditions she pines for.

Jolene and Carlos may not be a great success as a

family, but in many ways their informal association is as much of an achievement in New York, where the culture tends to pull families apart, as the Bylers' marriage is in Big Valley, where families are clamped together in a vise of religion and tradition. Jolene and Carlos have tried hard to improve Macy's life. Although they are not lavish they don't stint on her wardrobe. She has a sizable record collection, a shoebox full of baseball cards (she's a Yankee fan), a library of paperback books (her teachers praise her reading skills), and a big four-poster bed with a white sateen canopy suitable for a princess, or a Sleeping Beauty. Although Jolene is not fully attuned to her daughter's pain, she makes an effort to shelter Macy from the undesirable influences of life in New York. She talks to her about boys, about the ugly things that can happen on the street, about how to handle herself in an emergency. Jolene tries to help her daughter cope, but she knows she can't protect her from randomness.

On the walls in Macy's bedroom, beside her astrology chart, are two pictures of her real father, Lamar Mizell, one a hand-colored print of his high-school graduation photo taken in Goldsboro, North Carolina. In his glasses and mortarboard he looks genial and scholarly. The other picture is a charcoal sketch in profile, done by a sidewalk artist shortly after Lamar arrived in New York. In this portrait his hair is longer and his glasses are missing, and he's sporting a mustache and a goatee: he is the dead man of Macy's dreams, on the sofa in a room full of devils.

In her dreams he is already dead. In her memory, or else her imagination—not her dreams—he is an extremely tall man (for Macy was only three when she last saw him). He is standing in front of her, arguing with another, much older man. Macy watches them from her bed. They are struggling at the window. The older man is trying to push Macy's father out of the window, but he can't; Lamar is strong and he's braced himself. The older man runs to the kitchen and Lamar runs after him, out of Macy's sight, out of her life. "I don't think she remembers, but she wishes she could have," says Jolene. "Because what she remembers ain't exactly what happened. I didn't see him get the knife. Macy's father grabbed him in a bear hug, and I don't think he saw it either. When we pulled him up he was already cut. I put a dishtowel on his chest, and when I moved it I could see his heart. He was dead before the police came. Macy is the only daughter of Lamar Mizell. He was killed by his very own father."

# Chapter 12

Sunday School for the second-grade-going-on-third met
in the basement of the Walnut Grove Mennonite Church
under the direction of Wilma Yoder, reputed to be the
most efficient and conscientious teacher in the church,
with a confident manner that makes the children respect
her. Wilma has a sharp, thin face and wears black glasses
that slant down toward the bridge of her nose. Her hair
is battleship gray, and sweeps up from either side into her
capacious devotional covering. She sat with her hands
folded in her lap waiting for the bell to ring. Beside her
was a large box of teaching materials that she had pre-
pared to illustrate the lesson, "God's Friends Stand
Firm," based on the story of Daniel in the lions' den.
This evening Wilma noticed that her second-graders
were stirred up by the presence of three Fresh Air children. She made a point of learning their names: Rita
Cruz and Julio Ruiz, both from the Bronx, and Donny
Perez from Bedford-Stuyvesant. They would probably be shy at first and Wilma would need to encourage
them.

"Did everyone learn his Bible lesson for today?"

The children were still fooling around when the bell
rang, shuffling their small chairs back and forth. Through

the curtain that separated the second grade from the first wafted the lugubrious strains of "Yes, Jesus Loves Me." Glenn Kauffman, Donny Perez's host, identified the Bible verse as "We ought to obey God rather than men." Glenn wore a tee shirt promoting Holstein cattle. Like the other local children, he was barefoot. On the right side of his head were four bloody stitches from his latest bike accident, that afternoon.

"Right. And where is it found? It's found in Acts 5:29, isn't it?"

After the children read their lesson, Wilma passed out cardboard cutouts of Daniel for them to paste into their books, a reinforcement exercise recommended by the teacher's manual. Julio held the Elmer's Glue above his head and squeezed a long white string onto the page, watching it ooze into the center margin. Donny asked if he could go to the bathroom.

"Yes. Julio, can you say your Bible verse?" Wilma was staring at the figure of Daniel, forlornly afloat on the lake of glue.

"It's *Hu*lio," he said, sticking out his lower lip and giving Wilma a phony indignant look. Julio is a black-eyed, curly-haired Puerto Rican. A bull elephant rampaged on the front of his tee shirt.

Wilma smiled apologetically, but with a firm look in her eyes so that Julio would realize that cheeky behavior isn't tolerated. "Well, *Hu*lio. Why didn't the lions eat Daniel?"

"Angels shut them lions up!"

"Right. Most people wouldn't have angels with them, and the lions would have eaten them, but Daniel had angels with him and the lions' mouths were shut."

"Wilma, my cat died," said Leslie, a pigtailed blonde in a plain cotton dress.

"Big deal! Three of my puppies died!" Glenn cried irately.

"Rita Cruz, can you say the Bible verse? Julio, sit down."

"Can I go to the bathroom?" asked Leslie.

"Is it really necessary?"

Leslie nodded emphatically. Rita slipped out with her. Donny returned and played with the glue. "Aaach! I'm bleeding white blood! What are you doing going barefoot?"

"Everybody goes barefoot sometimes," said Julio. His feet felt funny and cold on the linoleum tiles.

"Turn to page forty," said Wilma, but she couldn't seem to get the attention of the class. Most of them were watching Julio eat glue. Pearl, the teacher's pet, sat next to Wilma and harrumphed indignantly.

"Does everyone know his alphabet? Everyone be quiet now. Julio!"

"Julio!" echoed Pearl.

"*Hu*lio!" Donny roared. Julio giggled.

"Page forty! See where it says, 'A promise from God for _____.' Fill in your name in the space. We're going to decode a message from God."

In the children's books was the message: GFBS UIPV OPU; GPS J BN XJUI UIFF: CF OPU EJTNBZFE; GPS J BN UIZ HPE: J XJMM TUSFOHUIFO UIFF; ZFB, J XJMM IFMQ UIFF." JTBJBI 41:10. "You see all these letters?" asked Wilma. "You write in the blank below each letter the letter that comes just before it in the alphabet."

The children bent down and began to work.

"What comes after O?" Donny inquired.

Pearl leaned over and examined Donny's answer, which began HGCT VJQW. "Look at what you've done!" she chided. "You've got it all wrong!" Pearl frowned in admonishment. Two long yellow braids hung down her back.

"I'll put glue in your mouth," Donny warned her.

"You little rascal," said Rita.

"Donny, do your work now."

"I'm hot. Can't I get a drink?"

"Do your work first."

"I don't know *how* to do it. This is my first time being here." Donny crossed his hands over his book and watched the others work.

A large boy named Jimmy with strawberry-blond hair and a face splattered with freckles studied Rita Cruz. "Wilma, she's got BBs in her ears!" he complained.

"They're pierced, dummy!"

"Leslie, what happened to your pencil?"

Leslie looked baffled. "I was just talking and . . ." She threw up her hands. "Can I have another one?"

"You'uns got about five minutes and then you've got to finish it at home."

*"Oh, no!"*

"What goes before A?" asked Julio.

"I'm going to the bathroom!" Glenn said on his way out. Donny jumped up and joined him before Wilma could say anything.

"Can I go, too?" asked Rita.

"You just went!"

"No, I didn't. I *went,* but I didn't—"

"All right," Wilma snapped. She sighed, feeling an unaccustomed tension in the cords of her neck. She referred back to her teacher's manual. "After they finish decoding the verse, read it together," it advised. "Talk about the words 'thou' and 'yea.' Tell them those are Old English words. 'Thou' and 'thee' both mean 'you.' 'Yea' means 'yes.' Also talk about what it means to be dismayed."

Wilma knew what it meant to be dismayed.

"When are we gonna have snack?" Pearl whined.

"First we're going to read the exercise. Okay, let me go ahead and read it for you. It says 'Fear thou not; for I am with thee: be not dismayed; for I am thy God: I will strengthen thee; yea, I will help thee.' Isaiah 41:10. Now, who can tell me what 'thy' means?"

"It's part of your leg," said Julio.

Pearl rolled her eyes. "It means *'yourself,'* " she groaned.

"Oh, really?"

"Rita, what does 'yea' mean?" Wilma asked.

Rita Cruz was just returning from the bathroom. She looked blank. *"Yea?"*

"Back in Bible times," Wilma coached her. "It's an Old English word."

"What do you mean what does it mean?" Rita wiped her hands on her blue tee shirt, which advertised the magazine *Oui.*

"It means 'yes,' " Wilma said testily.

Donny and Glenn came back and sat down, whispering and giggling. "This isn't working out this way," Wilma decided aloud. "Glenn, I want you to change places with Pearl."

"I wanna sit by Donny."

"Oh, honestly!" Pearl snorted.

"No, you two have to sit separately."

Pearl closed her book in disgust and walked around the table, martyred to the cause of good behavior.

The manual advised Wilma to teach the children to sing "All Night, All Day." "This is a simple tune with simple words. It will bring comfort to your second-graders, if you take the time to teach it," the manual assured her. "Sing it for the children several times. Let them join you and sing it together several times. Then ask, 'When does God watch over you?' Let them sing the answer:

*'All night, all day!*
*Angels watching over me, my Lord!' "*

Glenn belched. "I couldn't help it," he explained. From across the table Donny threw a wad of paper in his face.

"When're we gonna have snack!"

Wilma capitulated. She left through the curtain and returned with a tray full of Pringles and malted-milk balls, and a pitcher of orange Kool-Aid.

"I don't need juice after drinking his blood," said Julio, looking at Jimmy. "I'll get you when we go outside. Mmmmm!" Julio rubbed his tummy and smiled, showing his teeth.

"You won't get him, he's my friend!" said Glenn.

"He won't be your friend no more when he's in my stomach."

"You're not going to eat him!"

"I'm going to eat you, too. Then you can play in my stomach!"

*"Disgusting,"* said Pearl.

Glenn noticed a shoe sticking through the bottom of the curtain from an adjoining fourth-grade class. It was an orange Roman sandal. He walked over and stepped hard on the toe and smiled at the yelp that followed.

Tyrone Howard burst through the curtain. "You wanna fight, Jack?"

A huge female arm looped around Tyrone's neck and drew him back into the fourth-grade compartment.

"Glenn! Do you want to sit down here? Then you

behave." Wilma's voice had gone high and frail. Her crisp demeanor was crumpled. She examined her teacher's manual feverishly.

"If the children seem restless, use the exercise 'Trees in the Forest,' " it advised.

"Okay, everybody up! Put your hands over your heads and stretch! We're going to do 'Trees in the Forest.' Where's Donny?"

"I'll find him!" cried Rita, slipping under the table. "Get out of here, you little rascal!"

"Get out yourself! I'll put glue in your pants."

"Everybody stand up! Please! Please?"

"Can I go to the bathroom?"

"You've already been. Three times!"

Something got Glenn's leg. He struggled briefly in his chair, then disappeared under the table.

*"Everybody stand!"* Pearl screamed.

Jimmy slowly drew the table aside, revealing Julio, Donny, Rita, and Glenn wrestling on the floor. Leslie threw the bottle of glue on the pile, hitting Glenn on the side of his head where stitches were. Blood seeped out and puddled on the linoleum. Suddenly the bell rang and the class evacuated, leaving Wilma alone in the wreckage of her classroom—amid the blood and glue, the malted-milk balls, the supplicating Daniels, the overturned chairs and broken pencils, the discarded teacher's manual —her eyes closed and her arms upraised, swaying slightly in the aftermath like an old tree in a gust of wind.

# Chapter 13

Wednesday is market day in Big Valley, the one day that farmers may find a little time to sell their livestock or scout the prices at the Belleville Sale Barn, which is located behind the Citgo station in the center of town, one block down from the First National Bank. The auction is a non-sectarian social occasion; it breaks up the cultural monotony of the rest of the week, and even a farmer in the middle of harvest may look for an excuse to put in an appearance. His family usually comes along to enjoy the outdoor flea market that has grown up outside the Sale Barn. His wife may mention the need for bananas, which are not a difficult commodity to find in the valley, although the association of bananas with the Sale Barn is so routine that a visitor might guess that the market had been cornered.

For the Amish especially, Sale Barn day is a good time to mix with English people, or to encounter strangers from outside the valley. With all that is said about the curiosity of tourists about Amish habits and dress, at the Sale Barn the situation is reversed. Amish fathers take particular pleasure in leading their gaping children past tables of cheap merchandise and nodding in the direction of the fat lady in a baseball cap, with pink shorts and varicose veins, or the barking "antique" dealer with a cigarette dangling from blue lips—sights worth a thousand preachments on the consequences of worldliness. There are the additional delights of finding an odd tool and haggling over its price (a Levantine pleasure among the Amish), or of dining on a slice of pizza and a snow cone. On a hot day there will also be women in halter tops and men without shirts. There may even be some loose language, so some people avoid the Sale Barn because it's just too risqué.

Esther Peachey refuses to go because of her bad associations. Once when she was pregnant with Galen she passed a man smoking a thick cigar and she fainted dead away. Another time, a friend who ran a lunch stand got involved with the fruit seller and left her husband. Now Esther can't go near the Sale Barn without thinking of tobacco and adultery. So on Wednesdays, when her children insist, she drops them off at the Citgo station and they always find a ride home.

With Tyrone and Galen in the car, she had to stop this Wednesday at the bank to cash a check in order to pay Galen his weekly allowance of seventy-five cents, and a dollar to Tyrone for washing the car. Altogether, Tyrone would have $1.10 to spend, including a dime he had found on the floorboard, and Galen withdrew an additional thirty-five cents from his piggy bank so he would have an equal amount. The boys followed Esther up the marble steps of the First National Bank and continued to circle in the revolving door until Esther snatched them out. She stood at the teller's window while Tyrone fiddled with the deposit slips and changed the day's date on the calendar.

Beside the door in a folding chair sat Froggy McPhee, who often finds respite in the air-conditioned lobby from the mid-morning summer sun. Galen noticed him immediately. In the minds of many children in the valley, Froggy is the bogeyman. He is what gets you if you don't behave; he is what you become if you drink and smoke and follow the passions of the world. At night, when children rehearse their fears before falling asleep, Tyrone talks about monsters and Martians and Galen talks about Froggy. But Tyrone's apparitions never catch him by surprise in broad daylight in public places. Froggy is in his late sixties, with a frazzled crew cut in an ashy shade of gray. His eyes, which are narrowly spaced, are dull yellow globes with brown stains in the centers, like burned-out light bulbs. His body is crimped and twisted. He wore shiny gray pants and a flannel shirt, one sleeve flapping empty and the other rolled up over a thin arm blotched with liver spots and blue with tattoos. In a torn shirt pocket he kept a foil of tobacco, which he now tapped into a paper and rolled into a cigarette, one-handed.

Tyrone nudged Galen. "That Froggy?" He had recognized him from Galen's nightly tales.

"Shh."

"Hey, Froggy!" The marble walls amplified Tyrone's naturally loud voice. "It true you wrote a book?"

Bank business halted at once. Of all the lore and gossip that had accumulated around this exceptional figure, the rumor of Froggy's book was the most frightening. Since almost no one talked to Froggy, beyond an ironic good-morning-nice-weather, his purported book had swollen into a local legend, greatly inflated by the horrible thought of what he might have written in response to all the sermons that used him as an object lesson. Froggy gave Tyrone a startled, unfocused look.

"Yeah, I wrote one," he admitted.

"What about?"

"Oh, this and that." Froggy looked to Esther for help, but like everyone else in the bank she was paralyzed with curiosity.

"How much they pay you for it?"

"Nothin'. Nobody paid me nothin'."

"Where is this 'book'? You got it on you?"

Froggy squinted. "It's in Philadelphia."

Tyrone sneered. "I can't believe you wrote a book for *nothin'!*"

Froggy stood up—with his question-mark posture he was head to head with Tyrone—and announced that he was going to eat. He walked outside and confronted the sunlight. Tyrone pursued him through the revolving door.

"You got a house?"

Froggy shook his head no.

"Then where you sleep? In the street?"

"Oh, overheres," Froggy mumbled vaguely, hobbling out of range as quickly as possible.

When Esther and Galen came out Tyrone was shaking his head in disgust. "He ain't drunk," he snorted. "He stink. He the town stink. He got dirt all in his chest. P-U! You would die if you take a little whiff of him."

"I don't know how the poor man lives," said Esther.

"He got money," said Tyrone. "He got tens and twenties. He ain't wrote no book for free. I axed him when he wrote the book and he said, 'Many, many years ago.' You see them tattoos? Man, he musta been in the army a hundred times!"

"Thelafa firlafirst nalafash olafo nalafal balafank oflafof kilafish ilafi colafo quillafill lalafas."

"What's that?" asked Macy.

"The First National Bank of Kishacoquillas." Anna

Louise pointed out the structure on the right as they rode to the Sale Barn. "Oh, there's that old man! Did you notice?"

"Who?"

"This old man, he just sits along the street and looks so, ahh, *sickly.* Mom says he drinks and smokes all the time!"

"Doesn't even eat!" said Rose. "Just sits on the steps with his head down. They say he wrote a book, and that's where he gets all his money for cigarettes."

Macy nodded. "You know Farrah Fawcett-Majors? She's terrible good on a skateboard. She's on this show, it's called *Charlie's Angels,* and she gets like $25,000 an episode. And it comes on every Wednesday night. And she wants $150,000 a show! So they're going to sue her."

"Hm," said Anna Louise.

Norm Kanagy maneuvered a truckload of pigs through the flea-market crowd to the rear of the big tin Sale Barn, which mirrored the hot shine of the lunchtime sun. As he backed into the livestock pens D.J. and Drill hopped off the back of the truck and ran upstairs to the catwalk across the rafters. Under the tin roof of the barn the air was like a furnace. Below they could see the pigs being goaded through the labyrinth. Norm came behind them, and as he passed below the boys he removed his Pioneer Seed cap to wipe his forehead. His hair lay in wet black curls. When the pigs arrived at their allotted cage they were immediately hosed down. They don't sweat, Drill had explained, so they need the water to lower their body temperature.

The boys followed the catwalk down to the auction pit, steeply bound on three sides by unpainted bleachers, polished to a keen shine by the agitation of denim overalls. An overheated auctioneer with an open shirt wet a handkerchief with Seven-Up and mopped his fleecy chest. Behind him, above the dais, there was a wall of framed advertisements for Goss Fertilizer, Fultz Farm Equipment, and H. L. Peachey Custom Slaughtering. D.J. watched a Holstein cow with a heavy udder plod around the sawdust arena. "How can a bull give milk?" he asked.

"That's no bull."

"A cow with horns? Your cows ain't have horns."

"'Cause we cut them off."

When the Holstein sold, a man next to the auctioneer clipped the invoice to a rope which ran over the heads of the audience to a pulley in the sales office in the rear. Above the gate, a light flashed the weight of the next animal on the block: 620 pounds, a young Red Angus steer. Two hostlers with electric prods paraded the animal around the pen. The auctioneer lubricated his vocal chords with a prolonged sip of Seven-Up and began his spiel, acknowledging the nods and twitches from the gallery of overalls above him. He worked the price up to 25¼ cents per pound—a little over $150 for about 300 pounds of usable beef. D.J. tapped his pencil on his knee, keeping the beat of the auctioneer's chant. The next animal, a black-faced sheep, sold for 42 cents a pound. D.J. yawned in the heat and said he was going outside.

"Aren't you gonna wait for Dad's pigs?"

"I ain't no pigodometrist. And I don't love flies, neither. I'm slightly prejudiced in that direction."

"About half too much, in my opinion."

On his way out, D.J. ran into Luke Peachey, who was in the market for baby ducks. Franklin Williams was with him, in his Yankees hat and blue-striped jogging shoes. When he got the fly report he decided to join D.J. in the flea market.

Outside, Franklin pointed to a group of Amish boys in mauve shirts and straw hats who were mouthing "Fresh Airs" to each other. "One thing I don't like about Ammies—they stare at you. See 'em givin' us the hairy eyeball? I'm gonna stare right back!"

"Don't flash your money," D.J. joked.

"They think we look funny. They look worse than we do. Hey! Them shoes gotta go!" Franklin pointed to the rounded boots the Amish boys wore. "I'm glad I'm not Amish. I couldn't wear the clothes. They wear the same clothes every day."

"They smell."

"Hey, Chico! Find what you're lookin' for?" Franklin hollered. "Better not come to Brooklyn! You'd get killed!" He laughed, then said in a low, sarcastic voice, "But I wouldn't kill them. I'm too *nice.*"

"If my cousin be here, he has to hurt somebody before he go," D.J. said furiously.

"See, that's how I am. I can't stand somebody starin' at me. When I first come, Luke thought I was a rotten guy 'cause I was throwin' rocks at people. But I told him I was a Christian."

"You look like Jerry Lewis!" D.J. shouted at the astonished Amish boys, who quickly turned around and headed in another direction.

"Jerry Lewis!" Franklin said. "Ha! They really did! Stupid Ammies!"

"Did you watch Jerry Lewis Week?" asked D.J.

"It was really bad! You see *Cinderfella?*"

"It was butch!"

"And *Hollywood or Bust*, with Jerry Lewis and Dean

Martin! Them two used to be partners, like Abbott and Costello."

"You know what I like? When Abbott and Costello got stuck on the moon—"

"Yeah! When they came back they almost hit the Statue of Liberty!"

"You watch *The Honeymooners?*"

"Heeey, Ralph!" said Franklin.

They went on, as they walked through the flea market, calling out old television shows that are now repeated on afternoon television in New York. Just the mention of an episode was a kind of shorthand storytelling.

"Yeah! *The Flintstones*—the time Fred Flintstone wakes up twenty years later."

"Yeah. It was called 'The Late Multi-Millionaire, Mr. Rubble.' "

*"The Life of Riley!"*

"I can hardly wait till we get back."

The flea market stands were set up on old card tables or on the tailgates of station wagons, supervised by sunburned merchants in lawn chairs. A man with a leather visor and no shirt watched distrustfully as Tyrone handled a ten-dollar music box, on which a pink ballerina revolved to a theme from *Swan Lake.*

"That's nice, Jack!" Tyrone told him. "I had that playin' aroun' me when I was a baby. Every night! That's beautiful, man!"

Galen studied a rusted steel leg trap. In the winter he planned to set a trap line behind his house.

"Five dollars."

Galen set the trap aside.

Tyrone asked the price of a 30.06 rifle in the back of the salesman's station wagon.

"One-sixty-five."

"One dollar and sixty-five cents?"

"One hundred and sixty-five dollars." The man laughed. "Here, I got something I'll sell you for a buck." He showed them a homemade pop gun, "made from an elderberry branch," which fired a cork tied to a string.

"Don't want no *phony* gun."

"How 'bout this item?" The salesman produced a bottle of rose-scented perfume. "That sends you, don't it?"

"Mmm, that's nice!" Tyrone agreed. "But I really come to buy a puppy."

The salesman watched Tyrone drift into the crowd. "He wants a *what?*" the salesman asked the lady in the next booth.

"Puppet," she said.

Donny Perez bought a battery-operated burp gun that made a noise like a pneumatic drill. His host, Glenn Kauffman, bought one as well, although he wasn't sure what his mother would say when he brought it home (she doesn't allow toy guns in the house). The boys moved through the crowd, mowing down conversations twenty feet away with the incredible clatter of their guns.

"C'mon, lemme see that," said Julio Ruiz. Julio didn't have any money.

"No."

"You punk!"

Donny noticed a popcorn popper and went over to examine it. Julio studied a brass compact, a souvenir of Philadelphia. He examined a cigarette lighter in the form of a miniature lampshade.

"That's three dollars and fifty cents," said the woman behind the booth. "It was made in what they call Occupied Japan."

Julio saw a tray advertising the G. F. Eichenlaub Coal Company, with a painting of a Gibson Girl bathing in a moonlit lagoon. Julio touched her startled face.

"Where she get everything from? The attic?" asked Donny. He was trying on a plastic wristwatch with a flashlight in the dial.

Julio crossed his arms and strutted in front of the table. "If I got money, I'd buy everything here!" He gestured to the eggbeaters and bud vases and padlocks with unknown combinations. "I'd buy that and that and that!"

"Then you'd be rich!" said Donny.

The saleswoman noticed the furrowed expression on Glenn's face. "Can I help you with something, honey?"

Glenn nodded and handed over a quarter for a plastic whistle, which said, on one side: ELECT McCORKEL AUDITOR GENERAL, WILLIAMS STATE TREASURER. And on the other side: BLOW THE WHISTLE ON RECKLESS STATE SPENDING.

Macy and Rose were shopping for a birthday present for Anna Louise, who lagged discreetly behind so that they could confer. Rose looked fretfully at the booty spreading across table after table, and clutched a black change purse with both hands.

Macy admired a toy steam iron with a hole in the top. "It's for little flowers or an ashtray," she decided. "How much?"

"I usually sell them for a dollar," said a heat-flushed woman in a straw hat, "but since you ask, seventy-five cents."

Macy put it back. "I only got sixty-three cents. Oh, well."

"Are you from the City?" the woman asked.

Macy nodded.

"And you wanted something to take back to remind you of the country! Here," said the woman, handing over the plastic iron as a present.

Macy smiled cynically. Several feet from the stand, she said to Rose, "That's the advantage of being black!"

"Maybe I should dye myself," Rose said, impressed.

Macy bought a strawberry snow cone for a quarter. In a glass case Rose found a bright copper mouse, but it was overpriced. Macy picked up an old tin cigarette case from a table of antiques. It said, TOP—A PERFECTLY BLENDED CIGARETTE TOBACCO.

"It's a shame I spent my money. A pitiful shame. 'Cause now I got only thirty-eight cents left." She showed the case to Anna Louise.

"Just the thing for Carlos," Anna Louise said meanly.

Macy set the case down. That her mother's companion smokes is as much of an embarrassment to Macy as the fact that he lives unmarried in her home. Anna Louise and Rose also tend to give the vices equal weight. Macy picked up a heavy black globe with three holes in it.

"What is it?" asked Rose.

"A bowling ball. Here, put your fingers in it."

"I don't want to! We got to get something for Anna Louise!"

"Oh, yeah."

They watched Anna Louise admire a jewel box in the shape of a baby carriage. It was blue (Anna Louise's favorite color). She set it back on the shelf with pointed reluctance and moved to another booth.

"Four dollars and twenty-five cents!" said Rose when she found the price tag.

"Ooh, we can't afford that!"

"Maybe we should find her a dish. She always likes pretty dishes."

"This one," said Macy, selecting a red cut-glass candy bowl. The price was $1.25. They counted up their money, which was nearly a quarter short.

"Miss, is it all right if we give you a dollar for this?" Rose asked the saleswoman. "We're getting it for my sister's birthday. We've been hunting and hunting."

"Do you want to clean it?" asked the woman. She sprayed it with Windex and let the girls wipe it clean with a paper towel. It shone like a ruby.

*"Dange,"* said Rose, which is "Thank you" in Dutch.

"Dalafan gelafe," said Macy.

Galen led Tyrone to the rear of the Sale Barn, where the baby animals are sold.

"They better have puppies, Jack! I ain't heard a bark or a woof yet!"

There were cages of rabbits and chicks. Tyrone looked around despairingly. "Ain't you got no puppies? No cats neither?"

"They got little ducks," said Galen.

"Don't want no birds! I wanna buy a real animal! A chipmunk, or sump'm!" Tyrone groaned and left the barn, angry. "Why they keep all them animals in prison?" he complained. "If I had money I'd set 'em all free! Give 'em a fit home!"

Outside, the shadows were lengthening and the booths were shutting down. Desperately, Tyrone realized that he hadn't spent any of his $1.10. He saw a woman loading her wares into a plastic garbage bag. He snatched a Gillette Techmatic razor before she got it into the sack.

"How much is this?"

"A quarter," she said, a little stunned at the fury of his question.

Tyrone paid for the razor and rushed to another booth.

"You don't know how bad I wanna spend this money!"
he groaned. He bought a rusted Slinky for thirty-five
cents, and spent half a dollar on barbecue potato chips.
With a dime in his pocket he modeled an Amish straw
hat, and admired himself in the mirror of a compact. "I
look stylish in that," he told Galen. He put the hat back
on the table and spent his last dime on a package of
Bubble Yum.

Suddenly his eyes filled with frustrated tears. "Every-
time I get a dollar I don't get what I really want," he said.

"What do you want?" Galen asked.

"A tape recorder."

# Chapter 14

The Kore Peacheys grew used to waiting their meals for Tyrone to get out of the bathroom, where he spent hours operating on a cold sore or a loose tooth, or stuffing baby powder into his ear with a Q-Tip to "dry up" an earache. The night of Galen's birthday supper, Tyrone retired to the bathroom just before the cake appeared. Galen stared indignantly at the ten candles on his buttermilk chocolate cake, which slowly burned down into red puddles on the frosting. Outside a summer storm was thundering and thrashing trees in perfect correspondence to Galen's mood.

Tyrone made it hard to feel sorry for him, as Galen imagined he was supposed to since Tyrone was black and poor and lived in the city. Tyrone made these circumstances seem exciting and desirable, so that the pity Galen was trained to feel too often washed away in a quick flood of envy. He was overwhelmed by Tyrone. Tyrone bullied him, humiliated him. Tyrone took what he wanted without saying thanks. He sat in Galen's chair, he slept on Galen's side of the bed. He even appropriated Galen's dog, Prince, whom he called King. It was as if Galen had been displaced by a new, more vivid personality, and Galen himself merely trailed behind like a ghost, invisible in the glare of Tyrone's flamboyance.

Before Tyrone came, Galen and Prince would walk for hours in the woods picking blueberries and finding nests, so quiet they could come on deer and watch them feed. Now when they walked, Galen kept his hands in his pockets and his shoulders hunched as Tyrone and King charged after chipmunks, Tyrone with his arms and legs flying and his voice rising in hysterical roller-coaster shouts, and the dog excited to the point of nervous exhaustion so that he didn't seem to hear anymore when Galen called.

At night, when the lights were out, Tyrone started with the horror stories. "See, it was a dark, dark world with monsters in it," Tyrone said in his sinister, late-night-movie intonation, "and the only thing that could get away from monsters was a car. It had a tank of gas! All you could see was monsters. And a monster with green eyes and a ugly mouf came up and everybody was scared and they rolled up the window and he came closer —*thump! thump! thump!*—and he bust through the window and they stabbed his hand! He ripped the knife outta his hand and went on home.

"Late that night, the monster come back. *Thump! thump! thump!* He got one man outta the car. The man screamed a couple a times. The monster took him out in the woods and bit him in the neck and sucked his blood.

"Everybody be hungry. They ate dirt. They ate ants or crickets.

"Then the monster come back—*thump! thump! thump!* They had a BB gun in the car and they shot him in the head, *pow!* They started eatin' the monster eyes, and they ate his dead skin. And while they ate it they spit it on the ground. And then another monster came and ate everybody in the car! And when he ate them they all turned into monsters. But one of them didn't get ate, and he ran and he breathed harder and he turned into a monster. *Thump! thump! thump!* And he grew and then his blood was circulatin'! He went back to the car, got the BB gun, and day by day he ate monsters, *slurp, slurp.* Then one time, thousands of monsters came and they fight each other. Blood was flyin' out they eyes! And white blood and yellow blood and BBs shootin' and they looked at each other and AAAAAAAARGH!''

Esther came running in and turned on the light, finding Galen bolt upright and pale with fright, so that she thought it was he who had screamed. Tyrone was seemingly sound asleep and lightly snoring.

And yet when Galen finally did fall asleep he always slept securely, while Tyrone was trapped in the dark with his fabulous imagination. The night he arrived Esther heard him whimper and went to check on him, and found that he had wet the bed. "It was too dark," he moaned. "I couldn't find the baffroom!" The second night he called to her after midnight. "Cut the light on! There's a monster in my room!" Tyrone opened the drawer in the bureau and found a mouse trapped in the cellophane bag of potato chips he had stashed away for late-night snacks. "I thought it was a monster," he admitted sheepishly. "I thought I saw a eye shinin' at me, a monster eye. At first I thought it was comin' through the window, then I thought it was comin' through the wall. Then I thought it was bees. Then I thought it was a *mummy!*"

Galen fed the mouse to the cat, and Tyrone watched with remorse. He had planned to take the mouse home and train him.

After that episode Esther left a light on in the hall, but she still heard Tyrone fighting monsters at night. Without a TV set to irradiate the shadows, Tyrone seemed to be caught in a dreadful playback of his fantasies. Esther would come in and sit beside him and he would describe what had frightened him. "I had a dream! It was a lot of Martians, right? It was a machine gun in the room, right? Martians left it there. They kilt my bruvver, they kilt my whole fambly but my favver, and then they kilt him. I got the machine gun—it's powerful, it had a kickstand on it. And I shot every one of them down. All of 'em was fallin' all over the floor dyin'. They was green men with like a rocket head and had like little eyes and they had a flat nose with two holes in it and they was scary. And I was keep on killin' 'em and green blood started comin' out. Dead Martians was everywhere. Then a Martian cut the roof down and we fall to the second floor, me and the machine gun. I shot everybody and I was cryin' 'cause my bruvver was dead and they cut the floor again and we fell to the basement. Then they took me and they threw me in the rocket ship and we went to Mars. You woke me up just in time."

Tyrone would lie in bed and cry and Esther would hug him and comfort him. He told her how kids in New York teased him. "They make fun of me. They say I got dead eyes!" "You can't help it," Esther assured him; "God made you like that." "I know," said Tyrone, "I got eyes like my favver."

Tyrone finally came down from the bathroom and set a hammer and screwdriver on the table. "Tufe-ache," he explained.

"Now, Tyrone, don't tell me you been using them tools on your teeth!" said Kore.

"The dentist do."

"He does not!" Galen shouted, ready to make the most of it.

"Well, did you get it out, then?" asked Janet.

Tyrone shook his head no. "When we gonna eat?"

"We *could* have eaten half an hour ago!" Galen reminded him.

Tyrone was unusually equanimous tonight. He smiled as Esther put new candles in the cake and turned out the lamp so that the only light in the room, other than flashes of lightning from the storm outside, was a low orange glow that cast upward-slanting shadows on their faces. Tyrone was instantly cued. "Dark, dark night, the bogeyman out tonight!" His voice turned deep and husky. "The scene was in the baffroom. I have my cousin and friends over. I darken the place. I have this figure from a cereal box what glows in the dark, and I'm sayin' dark, dark night, bogeyman out tonight! It was Godzilla, Frankenstein, Dracula biting people in the neck. Then I pull out this figure and say RAAAAA! I ran into the bed! You could hear the screams echo in the street."

Galen stared at the table while the others laughed.

Esther clapped her hands fondly. "Oh, Tyrone! I bet you make the girls smile."

"I don't mess with girls," said Tyrone. "I don't like how they look, I don't like how they talk, I don't like how they be, I don't like them period."

"Don't you have girlfriends at home, yet?"

"No! With a girl, you got to test her out. Like a boy, he put some money on the table or food in the refrigerator. To see if she'll take it."

"Galen's had a date already," said Janet. "He went swimming with Cindy Esh."

Tyrone's lip curled. *"I can't stand to be in the water with girls!"*

Esther said Tyrone was the funniest boy she had ever met.

"When I grow up, I'mana be a comedy writer on Broadway," Tyrone admitted.

"That's quite an ambition!"

"How you gonna do that when you can't even write a letter to your mother?" Galen asked.

"Who says?" Tyrone shouted, but the point had been made. All week Esther had been urging Tyrone to write home, and finally he had asked if she would write it for him, and he would trace the letter in his own hand. That was the first that anyone in the Peachey family knew that Tyrone couldn't read or write.

In New York, Tyrone is enrolled in a class for neurologically impaired and emotionally handicapped children. The teachers there have assured Mrs. Howard that Tyrone is not retarded. His problem is perceptional: he just can't get characters on a page straight in his head. They come in all jumbled, like alphabet soup. Somehow Tyrone passed through four grades in the New York City school system before his problem was recognized. Mrs. Howard suspects that the source of Tyrone's affliction may be lead poisoning, which hospitalized three of her younger children. They were poisoned as infants from chewing on paint flecks in their disintegrating Brooklyn apartment to soothe the pain of teething.

Galen blew out the candles.

"Ten years old," Tyrone muttered. "I could be ten. Next time I come here I'll be ten. I could be ten today. I could have been born the same day my cousin was born, but the doctor say I'm too early to be born. I hate that man."

"Paul Harvey says anybody born today is a very special person," Galen bragged. "It's the seventh day of the seventh month."

"It be a special day anyway when you birthday come. A man should be treated like a king on his birthday."

"When is your birthday, Tyrone?" Esther asked.

"August the eleventh."

"In that case we'll just light the candles again and have *two* birthday parties."

That did it for Galen. Even his birthday was transgressed, the one day he shouldn't have to share with anyone. "I'm not hungry," he said when his mother handed him a slice of his favorite cake. She set it in front of him anyway. Tyrone ate three pieces. Afterward, Esther brought out Galen's present, a soccer ball she had purchased with green stamps. It was what Galen had asked for, and he was pleased in spite of himself.

"Here's something for you," said Kore, handing Tyrone a dollar bill.

"Oooh, *snap!*" Tyrone fanned himself with the bill.

"What will you spend it on, then?" Janet asked.

"Spend it on nasties. Popcorn, candy, maybe a tape recorder . . ."

"You ought to learn how to take care of your money," Kore advised.

"I will! One of these days I'mana get a lot of money, like five hundred dollars! I'mana take four of those hundred-dollar bills and roll them up in my sock, and spend a hundred dollars on toys and guns and stuff like that. A whole lot of stuff. Then with the second hundred I'mana buy food, a lot of canned goods. Then with the third hundred I'mana kinda go easy. Some furniture, a big sofa, a lawn. I'll grow a lot of things. Change it all into twenty-dollar bills, like sixty of 'em—"

"You'll have a hard time doing that!" said Galen. "There aren't sixty twenties in five hundert."

"How many then?"

"Guess."

"Thirty."

"How many twenties in a hundert?"

"How many?"

"I'm asking you."

Tyrone stared down at the smear of chocolate icing in his plate. Galen squirmed; he didn't like to see anyone humiliated.

But Kore was surprised. "Why, Tyrone, you can figure that! If I got two twenty-dollar bills how much is that?"

"Thirty."

Kore laughed, thinking that Tyrone was kidding. "How much is two plus two?"

"Four."

"So how much is twenty plus twenty?"

"Thirty?" Tyrone tried to count it on his fingers and came up with forty-seven."

"No!"

"Dad . . ." Galen cautioned, mortified that he had brought it up, now that his father was taking it seriously.

"Twenty and twenty is forty! Now I got three twenty-dollar bills, how much is that?"

"How much?"

"Three times twenty."

Tyrone didn't respond. Galen coached him under his breath, "Two—four—*six* . . ." but Tyrone was paralyzed. The numbers swam through his head. His mouth was partly opened and he sat with an expectant look on his face, as if an answer would surface like a burp and surprise him.

"Well, there are five twenties in a hundert," said Kore, "and if you have five hunderts that's five times five. Right? So what's five times five?"

"Leave him alone!" Galen sobbed, and ran from the table.

# Chapter 15

The shadow of Reverend Loren Hartzler danced in the light of the overhead projector. His sermon this Sunday was "Be of One Accord," and this injunction was ramified in four colors and projected on the bare wall behind the pulpit of the Mount Zion Mennonite Church. Some people in the valley, Reverend Hartzler intoned, take this injunction to mean that they must "wear the same clothes, farm the same way, paint their houses the same color"—and so on— *"instead* of being of one accord in the spirit of Jesus Christ!"

The congregation smiled at these oblique slurs against the Amish. It is a common Mennonite prejudice that the Amish are less spiritual than they, and that the Amish use of horse and buggy is less for the sake of God than for pure economy. Reverend Hartzler must be a diplomat when it comes to discussing schisms in the valley, however, for when he looks out from the pulpit he sees the beards and plain clothes of recent converts, and the cautioning eyebrows of many others in the congregation for whom the Amish heritage is too close for facile criticism.

Restless toddlers squirmed free and promenaded in the aisles during the sermon. Like the Amish, Mennonites believe in accustoming their children to church at an early age—although an Amish parent would be scandalized by the indulgence children enjoy in the Mount Zion Church, where sometimes the preacher can barely be heard over the squalls from the rear pews. And there is the famous tale of the Hartzler grandchild who wobbled all the way from the back of the church and climbed into the pulpit to sit on grandpa's lap.

Loren Hartzler is the patriarch of the Hartzler clan. His likeness smiles back at him in the faces of five children and over a dozen grandchildren among the churchgoers, most of them, like Luke Peachey, constructed on their grandfather's muscular prototype and with his wide mouth and slender nose, his close, deep-set eyes, and the distinctive Hartzler blink which signaled back and forth from preacher to flock like flashing lanterns.

Now Reverend Hartzler was steering the sermon toward his pet motif: how Mennonites are themselves different from the world, how they as pacifists are like the "defenseless Christians" of the apostolic church, "of one accord" on the Christian way of life but often not in accord with the rule of Caesar. His grandson Luke guessed what was coming next. "He's gonna tell the flag joke," Luke whispered in Franklin Williams's ear.

Reverend Hartzler chuckled. "It reminds me of the time a little Mennonite boy went to visit a church of another persuasion, and right behind the preacher they had all these *flags*. There was a flag of the United States, a church flag, and another flag with gold stars on a blue field. The boy asked the lady next to him what that flag was with the gold stars and she said it was to commemorate our boys who died in the service. The little boy thought about that for a minute, and then he said, 'The morning service or the evening service?' "

Luke groaned. "He musta told that joke a *million* times!"

When Mennonites felt out of step with the rest of the country in the past, it was usually over the question of war. Mennonites made up forty percent of the U.S. conscientious objectors in World War II, although they comprise only one-tenth of one percent of the total population. In most other respects they typified the idealized all-American white family, the Norman Rockwell family, deeply rooted in the protestant churches of America's small towns and rural communities, unaware of themselves as a class, living in the cloudless grace of the American bell jar. During the Vietnam War, however, the proportion of conscientious objectors who were not Mennonites rose enormously as pacifism became a political, not just a religious, issue. At the same time, America's image of itself radically changed. These days it is the traditional way of life—life as it is still lived in Big Valley—that is under attack. When members of the Mount Zion Church talk about worldly values they include not only violence, vice, and materialism but also divorce, abortion, sexual freedom, and women's liberation.

Through its missionary work the majority of the congregation is better acquainted than the average affluent American with the problems of the Third World, in all its gradations of misery from Biafra to the South Bronx. This knowledge has made the farmers more self-conscious about the abundance on their dinner tables. The grandly titled World Hunger Association (formerly, the Big Valley Relief Association) is the valley's own foreign aid program. Last year the WHA processed over a hundred cows into canned meat to send to places of need, along with garden vegetables and thousands of cakes of homemade lye soap. Many farmers, including Norm Kanagy, participate in the gilt project each year by sending a gravid hog to a poor farmer, probably a black farmer in Alabama or Mississippi, who keeps the litter and returns a gilt the following season. The church also sends volunteers through the Mennonite Disaster Service to clean up after calamities such as the 1972 earthquake in Nicaragua or the Johnstown flood of 1977. People in the valley still believe in neighborly charity, rather than governmental assistance.

Politics are almost never discussed in the valley, since no Amish and few Mennonites exercise their right to vote or hold public office. They are, by choice, unrepresented at any level of government. They believe that God orders society through its rulers, and that they should honor political leaders and obey the laws of the state as long as their conscience is not infringed upon. Richard Nixon was widely admired in the valley, in some part because of his Quaker background, and the corruption of his presidency became a lesson in the futility of mundane partisanship. Government, after all, is as inevitable and uncontrollable as the weather, and when it goes astray, like the weather, one can only pray for change.

Lately, most of the prayers on behalf of the government have been directed at the registered voters of the valley, who constitute a small percentage of its population but a clear majority of its drinkers. They voted to allow restaurants to serve beer, and although only one of the three restaurants in the valley has chosen to apply for a liquor license, the members of the Mount Zion Church see the vote as an inroad of the Devil. "If this goes on, brothers and sisters," warns Reverend Hartzler, "how will we be able to say in the next generation, 'Where do the heathen rage?' " But for all their unhappiness few Mennonites would even sign a petition to bring the matter to another vote. Instead they pray, they complain, and they boycott the offending restaurant, which continues to thrive off the business of thirsty Presbyterians.

Reverend Hartzler rushed to cover all the points in his outline, sounding slightly hysterical as he raced the clock. "Brothers and sisters, I get so *excited,*" he apologized in a cracking voice. When his sermon subsided he asked prayers for friends and relatives in the hospital, and for the speedy return of the Enos Hartzlers, the preacher's eldest son and his family, whose homecoming from the missionary fields in Colombia had been unaccountably delayed. Reverend Hartzler prayed loudly so he could be heard over the snoring of Tyrone Howard in the front pew.

Galen Peachey was sitting beside his mother, his face gone beyond red embarrassment to bloodless pallor. Tyrone was stretched out in the pew with his head in Esther's lap, making noises like a rooting pig, which generated giggles all over the church. Even Kore laughed, although he was only half awake himself. He looked down at Tyrone's feet in his lap and noticed several lumps in Tyrone's socks. Kore feared that they were boils, but Esther said, no, they were apricot pits.

After prayers the congregation sang "Onward, Christian Soldiers," and Esther's piercing soprano finally aroused Tyrone from his noisy slumber. He looked around sleepily, yawned and stretched, and when the hymn concluded he politely applauded.

Galen's features froze in a deathly grin. After church

he walked mechanically behind his parents to the car, refusing to sit in back with Tyrone on the way home. He didn't say a word, just stared at the sky through the window in vast reproach.

Kore asked Tyrone with some amusement if he had ever been to church before. "I been to lots," said Tyrone. "Every time I find one open, I go in."

# Chapter 16

The sad news reached the valley that Enos Hartzler was coming home from the mission fields with cancer. X-rays taken in Colombia showed that the malignancy was widespread and should be operated on at once. Enos insisted instead upon one day in Big Valley before checking into the Hershey Medical Center.

Luke Peachey didn't come down for supper. Quill knew that his son was up in his room thinking about his Uncle Enos, his idol since early childhood. Because of him, Luke had decided to become a missionary. Luke once imagined himself preaching to the Colombian Indians just as Enos did, but Luke's friendship with Franklin made him feel he had a different calling: to the Mennonite mission in the South Bronx. Few people in the valley, even those who had been years in the mission fields, had ever spent a full day in a major American city, and to Luke the Bronx was almost as exotic as the South American jungles.

Quill knocked on the door. "Son? You coming along?"

"I guess."

"They are expecting you."

The others were waiting in the car. They rode across the valley with Ann and Quill talking encouragingly about how good it was to have Enos home. Franklin didn't speak. For the first time on the trip he felt genuinely out of place.

Weeks before Enos and his family had been scheduled to return, his neighbors and relatives had fixed up his house and planted a garden. Now they stood in a circle in the living room, holding hands. Luke gasped when he saw his Uncle Enos, who had been the hardiest of all the athletic Hartzlers, being helped to the couch by his diminutive wife. Enos was shrunken and bent from his illness. He smiled sheepishly at Luke, but his eyes winced.

Franklin saw Darrell Jackson standing in the circle with the Norm Kanagys, and he smiled nervously in recognition.

Reverend Loren Hartzler stood to the side, both hands folded across his Bible, in downcast contemplation, eyes shut. He awaited the arrival of the Kore Peacheys before beginning the ceremony.

When they finally came, it was Tyrone leading the way. He bounded into the room oblivious to the grieved expressions, and sat on the couch next to Enos Hartzler. Enos laughed and introduced himself.

"This your place?" asked Tyrone. "You got it fix up real nice."

D.J. rolled his eyes.

Reverend Hartzler stepped into the ring of friends and read from James 5:14–15. "Is any sick among you? let him call for the elders of the church; and let them pray over him, anointing him with oil in the name of the Lord:

"And the prayer of faith shall save the sick, and the Lord shall raise him up; and if he have committed sins, they shall be forgiven him."

The Hartzlers in the circle blinked fiercely. "I've seen

it work already, brothers and sisters," Reverend Hartzler said in a quivering voice, "how sometimes the body is cured of disease, and sometimes not, but always *healed* in the sense that God calls you to Him, or lets you stay awhile on earth. I've seen before already where after an anointing service that spots didn't show up on X-rays. . . ." Reverend Hartzler's voice choked and he cleared his eyes with a Kleenex.

Then Enos spoke. He talked about how in the Colombian jungles he would read something in the Bible that struck him so profoundly that he would decide to preach on it, and within the very next week God would test him on it. He recalled that after he spoke on trusting in the Lord he noticed that the rain barrel in the camp was low and they would soon run out of drinking water, but when he set off down river to get an emergency supply it rained cats and dogs. It was the Lord's way of testing him; sort of a joke, really, to see if Enos believed what he preached. In his last sermon, Enos preached that fear of God is more important than anything, more important even than fear of life or fear of death. "Sure enough, I got it put to me rather abruptly. At first, I begged God to spare me. Now I'm resigned. The purpose of this ceremony is to place my case in the hands of the Great Physician, Jesus Christ. I just ask you to pray that if God does see fit to let me be cured, that I be able to use my life in His service."

Ann Peachey listened to her brother's gentle testimony and let the tears flood. But Luke would not cry. While Enos spoke, Luke looked away, with a hard-set, bitter expression—as if he had been betrayed.

The oil lay on the coffee table in a corked test tube. Reverend Hartzler lifted the pure, gold liquid overhead in a gesture like a toast, then poured it into his son's black hair. The elders of the Mount Zion Church stepped forward to lay their hands on Enos's head and pray. From the circle there was the sound of sobbing. Norm Kanagy reached up to wipe his face, and carried D.J.'s hand with him. D.J. felt the moisture on his hand and gulped.

After the ceremony Enos tried to catch Luke's eye, but Luke turned away and hid in the kitchen.

"I'm just real excited about the Christian life," Reverend Hartzler said afterward. "I feel relaxed now."

Franklin, Tyrone, and D.J. met outside under a maple tree. D.J. puffed his cheeks and sighed anxiously. "I never seen nothin' like that!"

"I have," said Franklin. "In my church we anoint all the time. Like three times a week."

"I mean the whole thing. Everybody cryin'. The way he looked."

"I feel sorry for Luke," said Franklin. "That's a bad thing for a kid to see."

D.J. agreed. "The worst thing I ever saw before that was my father dead in his coffin."

"I wonder how do it feel?"

"What?"

"To be dead."

"Chilly," said Tyrone. "It gonna be chilly 'cause when they put cement in you, it makes you cold."

"Cement!" Franklin cried.

"Cement, yeah. They put it in you."

"No, they don't! They *embalm* you. They take out your blood and they put perfumey stuff in. So you won't stink."

"No, they don't! They put cement in you!"

"No, they—" Franklin had to giggle. "Look. They take your blood and then they freeze you for a couple a days. They put you like in a drawer, or sump'm, and then they freeze you. And that's why you're so stiff. 'Cause when I kissed my mother when she died and was in the casket she was still cold."

D.J. and Franklin stopped laughing. The wound of parental deaths, so common in their neighborhoods, is a bond between them, rarely spoken of. They looked at the stunned and slow-moving relatives, a reminder of their own suffering when their bodies, too, had felt exhausted and leaden. Tyrone yawned.

"I saw a dead white person once."

"Huh?"

"When we was deliverin' telephone books in Queens."

"He's seen a dead white man!" Franklin said excitedly. "Where was he layin' at?"

"In the funerable parlor."

"What'd you do?"

"The only thing I do was looked at him. It was sad, but it couldn't do nutt'n to me, so why should I run off? I saw a man before I went in there and he said where you goin'? I said I wanna see that dead man. He said he ain't nutt'n to you. I said he might be. So I went in.

"They had pictures of God, a whole bunch of 'em. I started to take one home, but I didn't. It might bring bad luck—a dead person's things.

"I went in and touched it. He felt cold and hard. He was old and wrinkled and he had gray-and-brown hair. He wasn't scary. He had wrinkles right here." Tyrone pointed to his upper lip. "I told my muvver I saw a dead person in the funerable parlor. She said oooh, what's he look like? Wrinkled. He was old. Then we started back in the car deliverin' telephone books. When we was gettin' ready to go home my muvver bought a soda for us. And we drank it and went home."

# Chapter 17

It was the last day of the Fresh Air trip, and some of the families had gathered for a picnic supper on the ballground behind the Allensville Fire Company. After supper the men retired to the cool grass and lounged about, telling stories, while the young children crowded onto the ladder of the sliding board or launched themselves toward the stratosphere from their chain-link swings. The older children walked across an outfield of milkweed and dandelions to the baseball diamond. The women cleaned up.

"Whose broccoli dish is this?" asked Esther Peachey. "I'm gonna have to get the recipe!"

Martha Kanagy acknowledged that the broccoli dish was hers.

"What's in it? Cream of mushroom soup?"

"No, it's broccoli, rice, cream of chicken soup, and Cheez Whiz."

"Mmm! You think you could use Velveeta, yet?"

"I'm sure you could. I just keep Cheez Whiz in the cupboard most of the time. Darrell Lynn just loves it. Darrell Christopher does, too."

"Seems like those two got along real well this year," Ann Peachey observed.

"They really did. This summer Darrell Christopher's

been after me to teach him to sew. His mother has a machine in New York but I guess she doesn't use it. I told him I didn't have the patience! But I said I'd make him something, and he says, 'You know how to make a three-piece suit?' I told him I'd made Norm one. I got the material one Christmas and made the suit the next. And he says, 'It takes a *year* to make a suit?' Ha! But I finally did teach him to sew a straight seam. Now Darrell Lynn wants to learn, too."

"I wish Tyrone and Galen would get along," said Esther. "The other day we had watermelon at my mom's house, and Tyrone got mad and threw it at Galen and Galen threw the cat at him. Boy! Tyrone wasn't going to forget it! He said he was going to hit his head against the electric fence. And he went out in the middle of the field and oh, those big ol' tears came out of his big eyes. I said I was going to get Galen to apologize and Tyrone said, 'No, it's not good to apologize.' He says in New York when they have fights he just goes inside and plays sick."

"He's a strange boy."

"Every time he does something wrong he says, 'I made a mistake.' And I say, 'You sure did!' You just have to love him."

"Will you'uns be asking for him next year, then?"

"I guess not. It'll be up to Galen."

"The first time I asked colored Darrell if he'd do something in the barn he says, 'My ma paid four dollars for me to have fun, not work!' " said Norm Kanagy. He and the other men reclining in the grass were comparing the industriousness of their Fresh Air children. Most of them believe that city people hate work; the tacit assumption is that the reason people move to the city in the first place is to go on welfare, or else get a union job that is almost the same thing. "I told him if he pitches in I'd give him ten dollars when he goes home," Norm continued. "Now he's been working real good. He mows lawn, helps Darrell feed calves at night, helps unload hay. He said he was gonna use the money to buy cleats, jock strap, and an athletic cup. I asked what he needed with a cup and he says, *'Pro-tection,* man!' "

The men laughed.

"Ol' Franklin don't like to work, neither," said Quill. "When Luke was cleaning up the church one afternoon I told Franklin he'd have to do some chores and he says, 'I'll do anything, Dad, just don't make me feed the pigs!' "

"That Tyrone, now, he's a real worker," Kore Peachey declared. "Always asking for some job around the house. He got some of the neighbors to hire him picking apricots, already, and Lena Byler had him down to weed her garden two or three times. He says he's a gardener back in Queens."

"Yeah, but you know he can't have much of a life in New York," said Quill.

"I don't know. Tyrone keeps talking about all this free food they get."

"Free food?"

"Yeah, folks just lining up at mealtime and somebody hands 'em a dinner."

"No wonder the farmer can't make a living—if it's all free like he says!"

"Then he was saying about all these dogs down at the park in burlap bags. He claims people kill dogs at the parks in New York. He rides his bicycle around and counts the feet sticking out of the bags. I don't know if the kids in the neighborhood were having a contest or what."

"A city park!"

"It didn't seem likely to me, either," Kore admitted. " 'Cause if it's a city park, they must keep it pretty well cleaned up."

"Especially in New York, where they ain't got no other place for kids to play, no trees and such," said Norm.

"I don't know about that," said Kore. "The way Tyrone describes it, that Queens must be a beautiful place, with all them orchards and watermelon fields."

At the ballfield Franklin Williams was choosing his team, a process complicated by the presence of several girls and a pair of identical twins. It was already twilight. The sun had left the valley except for one field high on the opposite mountain, where shocks of wheat were tied up like yellow tepees, casting long late-afternoon shadows. The sky was blue with swirls of pink. Franklin puzzled over the choice of Jerry or Terry Barnes, a set of Presbyterian bookends attired in paisley Bermuda shorts.

"I guess I'll take Terry."

"No—Jerry!" said Glenn Kauffman. "He's better!"

"Okay, Jerry."

"Too late! Too late!" gloated Drill Kanagy, the captain of the opposing team. "You already picked Terry!"

Brooklyn's Gary Martin massaged his right hand, which was swollen from the knuckles to the wrist. "I hope Franklin don't put me in the outfield," Gary confided to D.J. "I don't think I can throw." He showed him his sore hand.

"What happened?"

"I hit that boy. Wow, he sure has a hard forehead." Gary pointed out the boy with the hard forehead, a local stalwart on Drill Kanagy's team named Willard Glick. Willard scowled back.

D.J. cast a nervous glance at Macy Mizell, who had seemed so feminine on the bus. Now she stood behind Drill wearing a New York Yankees hat, smacking gum and shifting her weight impatiently from hip to hip. She performed a few warm-up stretching exercises, which made D.J. worry. Where'd she learn to do that?

Anna Louise and Rose Byler were on Franklin's team. Although they frequently played softball after school with the other girls they had *never* played with the hard ball, or with boys. They were wearing their usual long-sleeved polyester dresses and their devotional coverings, and blue tennis shoes. Anna Louise sported a frazzled first-baseman's mitt.

Willard Glick introduced himself to Tyrone. "What's your name?" he asked.

"Trouble," said Tyrone. "But they call me Trub."

"What position you play, Trub?"

"Pitch."

"I guess not! I'm the pitcher on this team."

"I ain't playin' then."

"Hey, you guys!" said Drill. "No more of this arguing! Galen Peachey is the pitcher."

"Peachey can't pitch!" Willard complained.

"Can too!" said Galen.

Tyrone snorted and sat down behind the backstop.

Franklin's side was up first. After three hitters, Galen had walked one and hit two. The bases were loaded and nobody out. Willard Glick, who was catching, stormed out to the mound and demanded to pitch. Drill proposed that Willard and Galen trade positions. Galen accepted the catcher's mask and walked to the plate with his head down.

Franklin, batting cleanup, smacked a grand-slam home run over the outstretched glove of the right fielder. He trotted slowly around the bases in the shuffle-footed home-run style of Mickey Rivers.

"Does anybody here know *how* to pitch?" Drill inquired.

"I pitch girl's softball," said Macy.

Tyrone was already on the mound. "I pitch *baseball*, Jack. All the time!"

Tyrone took the ball and wound up in a huge motion. His first pitch was a ball high and outside. His next pitch hit the batter, one of the paisley twins, square in the back. The twin went sobbing down to first base.

Anna Louise Byler singled.

Rose Byler walked.

Gary Martin hit a double down the third-base line, between the third baseman and the runner standing on the bag, both of whom dived for cover; and since they happened to be the Presbyterian twins it looked like identical cell division.

The next batter walked.

The score was six to nothing, with the bases loaded and still nobody out. Drill made another trip to the mound. "We just had too many hits and walks," he apologized, taking the ball from Tyrone's hand.

"You know why? 'Cause you got a scrub team!"

"I'll say," said Willard Glick. "Look at our pitcher!"

"Yeah? I didn't see you catchin' any balls out there!"

" 'Cause you're walking 'em all!"

"Suck an egg, Jack!"

Drill put his foot down. "Now, that's enough! Tyrone, go to the outfield. I don't like nobody talking like that on my team!"

"Well, you ain't now 'cause I quit." Tyrone threw his

borrowed glove over the backstop and stalked off the field.

Macy pitched underhand just as she did in softball, in a high, slow arc, striking out Donny Perez. The next batter hit a dribbler toward first and was tagged out, although another run scored. D.J. sighed nervously as he came to the plate. He rubbed his hands with dirt and tapped the plate with his bat. The first two pitches floated across the plate like soap bubbles, and D.J. missed them both. The next one whistled past outside. Finally D.J. connected on a one-and-two pitch, sending a line drive directly at the forehead of the terrified twin on third, which he caught in self-defense. That retired the side.

Franklin laughed when his side took the field. He had a seven-run lead, but he wasn't taking chances. He selected himself as pitcher.

Drill Kanagy, the leadoff batter, singled; the next two men walked; and Galen Peachey hit a triple down the first-base line, right past Gary Martin, who just threw his glove at the ball as it screamed past.

"C'mon! Play as a team!" Franklin exhorted.

Tyrone seized a bat and walked to the plate. His left hand was above his right, so that he swung down with a chopping motion, and he waited to swing until the ball had popped into the catcher's mitt. He let go of the bat, and it narrowly missed the shortstop.

"*Whattaya doin'?*" Drill hollered.

"Whattaya think?" said Tyrone. "Strikin' out!" He swung wildly at two more pitches, sending his bat into the infield each time, then walked shamelessly off the field with his nose in the air.

"Doesn't count!" Drill contended.

"Does too!" said Franklin.

In a moment Franklin found himself with the bases full

again. There was a grim set to his jaw as he turned to look at his outfielders, who were sitting down in the settling darkness. "Hey, you guys don't even wanna play!" he complained.

Willard Glick hit a long fly ball to left field, and got to third before the ball returned to the infield. Luke walked; a twin struck out, complaining that he couldn't see the ball. Franklin had a one-run lead, two outs, and two strikes on Macy Mizell when Quill arrived to call the game on account of darkness.

"One more pitch!" Franklin demanded.

"Okay."

Franklin could barely see the batter, but he heard the crack when Macy hit it, winning the game and losing the ball, somewhere among the fireflies in the night-clad outfield.

# Chapter 18

Esther Peachey heard the muffled cry for help and rushed upstairs to Galen's room. It was empty.

"Help!"

She ran to the closet and opened the door. Tyrone was sitting on the floor with his legs crossed, blinking in the light. He had gotten locked in the closet while testing the Superman penlight Galen had given him as a going-away present. Galen had also given Tyrone a '37 Chevy model he had built from a kit and (at Esther's suggestion) his old *Children's Living Bible.* Tyrone stuffed them into his candy-striped laundry bag, along with a giant balloon in Day-Glo orange (ten feet in diameter when fully inflated), two Golden Rule pencils from the Mount Zion Church, a straw cowboy hat, a cactus seedling wrapped in moist tissue, and some canceled postage stamps that he had glued to his chest. In the morning the bus would come.

D.J. Jackson was packing his bag when Martha Kanagy came upstairs with his blue jeans from the laundry. "I found this tooth in the pocket," she said. "You want to take it home?"

"Nah, give it here. I'll put it under my pillow."

"I looked there three days ago and didn't find it. I

decided you didn't believe in the tooth fairy anymore."

D.J. smiled at the open mention of one of the frauds of childhood. "I was saving it for tonight," he kidded.

"She might not come back."

"I hope she does."

Drill read D.J.'s comic books for the last time. "Going home," he said glumly. He stretched across the bed with his chin in his hands. "It seems hard to believe."

"True."

"I wish you could come back before a *year*."

"Or you could come to New York. 'Specially since your mom and dad are excorting."

"They said they didn't want to have to take care of me, too."

"You could stay at my place. I got like a million comics."

"I guess I could bike up," said Drill. "If the bus makes it in six hours, I ought to be able to make it in eighteen."

"As if you could! You'll be like three days!"

"Not if I was to ride ten-speed."

"Well, if you come, come on Sunday and you can see me play football."

"Did you ever think what it would be like," said Drill, looking around at his familiar room, his too-familiar room, with ribbons from animal fairs and the Philadelphia Phillies pennant on the wall, the Hardy Boys books in the shelf, "if we was to trade places? And I'd be up in New York going to all them movies, and playing football, and you'd be feeding the calves every night and going to church every Sunday and the travelogue in Lewistown once a month."

"You wouldn't like New York."

"How do you know? I might!"

"If you was to come live in New York you be havin'

fights, like in school, and on the street lots of times. In New York, there ain't no garages, and you be drivin' around all the time wonderin' where to park. You can't be walkin' barefoot neither, 'cause your feet'll get cut on the glass. And besides, there ain't no cellar downstairs for you to go to."

"Yeah," said Drill, "but sometimes this place ain't so hot either."

In the morning Franklin Williams and Luke Peachey sat in the car waiting for Ann to drive them to the bus. Franklin hugged a tiny mimosa "sensitive plant" in his lap, which would stand on his windowsill in Brooklyn next to his brother's dancing trophies. Franklin stroked his finger across the leaves and they contracted at his touch. He had said hardly a word all morning.

"Maybe you could hide in the corn patch," Luke suggested.

Franklin grinned painfully.

"Or hide out on the mountain. Up where the crick comes out—nobody'd ever find you!"

"Nah." Franklin shook his head hopelessly. "Mom might get mad."

Ann finished her check of the house. "I guess you'uns got everything. Ready to go?"

Franklin stared at the cornfield. "I'll never be ready," he sighed.

All the way from the Bylers' driveway Macy could see the Greyhound awaiting her in the lot of the Mount Zion Church. It looked huge and out of place like a spaceship or a galleon, arrantly disregarding the parking stripes. Macy felt sick, as she had in her dream the night before she had come to Pennsylvania. She made a wish into the mouth of her hand-painted glass jar, which said BELLE-

VILLE, PA. across a spray of green holly. Her wish was that "I could live here forever." Although she was dressed in the same outfit she had come in, the tail of her designer tee shirt was not tucked in, to cover the fact that her rainbow jeans no longer fastened at the waist. In two weeks at the Bylers' her weight had swelled from 85 pounds to 103. Macy attributed the weight gain to the fresh corn on the cob, her favorite dish. The first thing that she will think to tell her mother, when she comes to pick her up at the Port Authority, is, "Mom, I wanna go back!" Then she will gasp when her mother snaps, "You can go back right now, for all I care."

Tyrone stood in front of the open bus door, wearing a powder-blue yachting cap, with his bulging laundry sack slung over his shoulder. He permitted Esther to kiss him, although he looked away as if he were getting an inoculation.

"Well, I guess we weren't too hard on you," she said, sniffing into a handkerchief.

"Oh, a little bit."

"What about you being hard on us!" Galen demanded.

"A little bit." Tyrone grinned.

Esther suddenly hugged him tight, tipping his cap to the side of his head. "I hope you'll grow up to be a good man," she said fervently. "I'll say a prayer for you."

"I don't mind." Tyrone adjusted his cap and boarded the bus.

"I don't know if we'll take him again," Esther remarked when Tyrone was gone. "The little stinker. After the way he behaved!"

Eddie Cato came on the bus with his hands crossed over his stomach to contain all of the packages of powdered white doughnuts he had stolen from the White Hall store. Ivan Stoltzfus had seen him do it. In fact, he had watched so carefully he had been able to count how many packages were taken, and would return on the way home to pay for them. He did not say anything when Eddie took them, but he felt like an accomplice. Any other child Ivan would have whaled across his knee, but Eddie had taken away his appetite for punishment.

D.J. Jackson installed a new pencil behind his ear, this one promoting Sire Power. He and Franklin had resumed their old seats next to the bathroom. Instead of his blue joggers, D.J. was wearing Drill's prized Converse sneakers, with the holes in the toes and a flapping heel. In a final gesture of friendship they had traded shoes.

"Did you ever hear of artificial simulation?" he asked Franklin. "Norm had three of his cows bred that way. He gets a frozen plastic thing and after it thaws out he sticks it up the cow's vagina, or whatever. I don't know what they call it on a cow."

"Why'd he do that?" asked Franklin.

"Once before they borrowed a neighbor's bull, right? And they put it in the room with the cow so he could jump her. And just when he was gonna do it, she moved. He almost stepped on his thing. That's when they called the man from Sire Power."

Franklin looked at his watch, which was set ten minutes fast. He jiggled his foot anxiously.

"It's not easy, goin' back," D.J. observed.

"Dad hugged me, told me to be a good boy, and do good work in school." Franklin chewed on his lip. "He always does that. But he know I can do it anyway."

The door closed behind Macy, locking her in with the other children captured in the dark corridor of the bus. Outside the green windows Rose and Anna Louise had already lost sight of her. They walked the length of the Greyhound, waving blankly at the opaque glass. With a great exhalation the bus released its brakes and entered State Road 655. Branches of the locust trees brushed the windows as it passed.

Macy slumped into her seat next to Gwendolyn Butler. Her eyebrows puckered and her bottom lip trembled. "Don't cry, Macy," said Gwendolyn, " 'cause you'll be seein' 'em next year."

At the mention of crying Macy burst into tears.

Gwendolyn patted her knee and consoled her by telling her how brave she was. That is, how brave Gwendolyn was. "I'm leavin' two cats back there. And a puppy! I had one cat already, named Nicole. This time I named one Juanita, after my mother. And the puppy I named Samantha. He cute."

Macy gagged. "I think I'm gonna throw up." She looked at her lap expectantly.

"Hey—what that lady's name in the song we was singin'?"

"Magdalena Pagdalena Rubensteiner Heinebeiner Hoca Loca Poca," Macy sobbed.

"Yeah, that's right. *She had two hairs, in her head. One was alive and the other was dead. Oh Magdalena Pagdalena Rubensteiner Heinebeiner Hoca Loca Poca was her na-a-ame!* What's the next verse?"

*"She had two teeth, in her mouth. One pointed north and the other pointed south."*

*"Oh Magdalena Pagdalena Rubensteiner Heinebeiner Hoca Loca Poca was her na-a-ame!"*

Gary Martin turned the tuner on his transistor radio, searching for a station. As soon as the bus left the valley and got up on the ridges signals flooded the dial. Gary's eyes were red and watery. "As soon as I get around hay, my nose fills up and my throat hurts," he explained. "I couldn't hardly sleep last night. They was makin' hay. But look." He held up the hand that had hit Willard Glick. The swelling had gone down considerably.

"I don't wanna go back to stinky New York," Rita Cruz complained. She clutched an autograph doll that was crowded with Mendozas and Hernandezes on one side, Bylers and Peacheys on the other.

Natasha Brown agreed. She was changed back into her tangerine jump-suit gauchos with the clear vinyl pockets, leaving her Amish dresses behind. "Big Valley is nicer than New York."

"That's the truth!"

" 'Cause in Big Valley we don't see a whole bunch a dogs runnin' around in the street gettin' hit and stuff. Like our dog name Herman got hit by a car."

"I like it here 'cause you can stay barefooted," said Rita.

"I'll say!"

"And in Big Valley, you be busy! You milk the cows, you get the eggs—in New York you don't do those stuff."

"I hate milkin' cows now," said Natasha. "When they be milkin' I be holdin' they tails so the cow don't get in they face. What you like so much 'bout milkin' cows?"

"You get paid."

The bus followed the rocky Susquehanna to Harrisburg, where it picked up the Interstate. The terrain flattened out and became familiar when the logos of gas stations and fast-food stores appeared. As they passed McDonald's the children began to sing, *"We do it all for you!"*

"You know something?" Macy was suddenly smiling at a memory. "We were sitting on the floor in Barbara Zook's playhouse and Anna Louise had on a pair of my jellies, right? And Barb's little brother says, 'You must be a black girl! I thought only black girls wear jellies!' "

Gwendolyn laughed.

"And I say, 'You ain't gotta be *brown* to wear jellies.' "

"That's right! If you gonna call us sump'm, don't say black!"

" 'Cause I ain't got no black on me."

" 'Cept for your hair."

"My hair ain't black. My hair is dark, dark brown."

"My hair is black *and* brown."

"I'd rather be colored. *Called* colored," Macy giggled. "Sometimes we girls be playin' in the car and one of them be sittin' here and I be sittin' in the middle and the other be sittin' here and I say, 'Oh, look at the sandwich!' I be lookin' both ways. 'You're the bread. I'm the meat, I guess.' "

D.J. was watching Macy talk to Gwendolyn—at least, he was watching the back of the seat where he knew she was sitting, and occasionally he could see a hand fly up in exclamation.

"When I get to New York I'm gonna call her up," he

announced. "We'll take in a movie. I'll wear my gabardines, my blue shirt with the designs on the back, and . . ."

"Sling Shots," Franklin advised. Sling Shots are tie-up suede shoes with gum soles.

"You be wearin' karate shoes," Tyrone suggested. "You look stylish like that." Karate shoes are black cloth shoes resembling ballet slippers.

"What do you know 'bout dressin' for a date?" D.J. sneered.

"A lot."

Franklin and D.J. looked at each other and laughed.

"I call girls!" said Tyrone. "I calls up lotsa girls. Take 'em to a game show. You don't b'leeb me?"

"Nope."

"I'll bet you. Dollar!"

"You ain't got that much in your pocket. You ain't even got no money in your pocket." Franklin had guessed right. Tyrone had spent everything on potato chips before getting on the bus. "Now if I was to go out," Franklin continued, "I would take her out to eat or, you know, I would go see a good Broat-way show."

"Like *Star Wars,*" D.J. suggested.

*"Superfly,"* said Tyrone.

"I'm talkin' about a *play.* A play!"

"Oh, a play."

"Like *Godspell."*

*"Godspell* is crazy," said Tyrone. "I seen it on TV."

"Shaddup! It is not! You should go see it, man!"

"Get outta here, man! You get that phony *Godspell* stuff and don't bother me. That *Godspell* stuff is corny."

"You don't know what you're talkin'," Franklin said angrily.

*"Godspell* ain't real! It ain't real!"

"You don't understand nutt'n! We know it ain't real,

but you don't understand . . . It's a *play,* stupid! You're not mature enough to understand things."

The bus crossed the Delaware River into New Jersey. The turnpike was choking in the diesel exhaust of heavy trucks bound for the city. Gary Martin was trying to pick up the news on WABC. Eddie Cato was in the toilet throwing up white-powdered doughnuts.

The highlight of his trip, Tyrone was telling Julio Ruiz and Donny Perez, was catching the mouse that ate his potato chips and feeding it to the cat. "Kitty was eatin' mice meat and drinkin' milk. All that blood was in the milk and he was drinkin' it." Tyrone licked his chops like a satiated cat.

Julio giggled wildly. An Amish straw hat sat on the back of his head like a sombrero. He carried an artificial iris as a present for his mother.

"Whattaya gonna do when you get back to New York?" asked Natasha.

"Nutt'n!" Rita exclaimed, disgusted. "I sit around doing nothing in the house."

"Right!" Natasha said happily. "Sleep! And watch TV! I watch TV a lot. I sit up too close, almost got blinded. I be layin' down on the couch eatin' popcorn, potato chips, pizza with garlic . . ."

"Mmm!"

"And I'm gonna get a pepperoni. I got seventy-nine cents, so I'm gonna go to the pizza shop and buy me a pizza and soda. A twenty-cent drink!"

Newark International Airport appeared to the left, behind the wavy prisms of airplane exhaust and industrial fumes. Franklin curled his lip at the iron-gray horizon. "When you're in the country with all that fresh air and then you come back, all that stuff gets in your lungs. Like the gasoline stuff and the trailer-truck smell—"

"And the ocean so dirty," said D.J.

"Violence, pollution, and gossip," Franklin pronounced. "That what's wrong with New York."

"People don't mind they business," Tyrone agreed.

"They don't hardly do that much stuff in Big Valley—have murders and robberies and other things," D.J. mused. "At least, I never heard of one." He looked bitterly at the passing refineries. "Some black people just like to fight, I guess. And go to parties and drink, get all high and start fights and everything."

"You don't like bein' black?" asked Tyrone.

"That's my color. Ain't nutt'n I can do about it. Whoever don't like it—I guess they just have to like it."

"Bein' black better than bein' a nigger," Tyrone assured him.

"You don't know what is a nigger," Franklin sneered. "You just a kid. You don't understand things."

"A nigger is a white person!" Tyrone exclaimed.

Franklin laughed derisively. "It's not only a white person—"

"Did I say it was *only* a white person?"

"A nigger could be anybody," said Franklin. "It's a liar."

"It's a liar, *and* it's a white person," said Tyrone. "And a black person is a colored."

"Then what's a yellah person?" asked D.J.

"They Japs. And I don't like them, period! 'Cause they kilt people durin' the war. I don't wanna change no colors bein' yellah or white. I wanna be myself. Like God made me."

"You don't believe in God," Franklin asserted.

"Yeah, I b'leeb in God," Tyrone said nervously,

knowing he had gotten trapped in Franklin's specialty.

"Like how? How you believe in God?"

Tyrone shut his mouth and toyed with his cap.

"Tell the man how you believe in God," D.J. taunted.

"I b'leeb in God."

"What is He? See, you don't even know what He is, do you? What is Jesus Christ to you?"

"He sump'm to me."

"What?"

"Save-yah."

"He's your Save-yah, He's your friend, He's your guide," Franklin lectured. "See, you don't even understand about Him? You don't know the Lord Jesus Christ, so just keep your mouth shut."

"Oh, boy! You think you know so much!"

"There's New York!" someone cried, spotting the spires of the city poking through the smog.

"Hooray!"

"I HATE NEW YORK!" Macy screamed.

"NEW YORK HATES YOU!" shouted Donny Perez.

Macy wheeled around and glared at him through tears. "Shaddup, your mother hates you!"

The bus sank into the Lincoln Tunnel, and forty hands simultaneously reached for the reading lights.

Some of the children, when they got home, would find their lives changed. Another building on Franklin's block had burned, probably the last weight in the scale for his neighborhood before it surrendered entirely. A friend of Natasha's, a girl who lived across the street and jumped rope with her, had been found in an abandoned building, stabbed to death. She had been raped. She was twelve years old. "Her mamma sent her out for burgers and she got kilt," is the way Natasha would explain it.

For most of the children, their stay in Big Valley would prove little more than a momentary calm in lives so abused by randomness. The Fresh Air Fund is sometimes criticized for giving some children who are caught in the ghetto impossible expectations for the future, and others a depressing understanding of how deprived they really are. As a matter of fact, this criticism is often expressed in the black community. And yet intelligent and sensitive children already know the truth of their situation. The difference that the Fresh Air Fund can make is not so much that they expect better, but that they realize they deserve better. For some of them, coming home is the beginning of a lifelong outrage.

D.J. listened to the horns resound in the bottom of the half-lit concrete tube, which burrowed under the Hudson River and surfaced in midtown Manhattan. "I wonder how they make a tunnel," he mused. "With all the water rushin' in one side?"

"They use a frogman suit," said Tyrone.

Franklin threw up his hands. "No, they don't! They use a submarine!"

# Chapter 19

"Mommy, we made tea! We picked the leaves, like mint, and I didn't like it, period! I fed it to the goats. These flies was after me, Ma! They was bitin' me like shame. I killed about eighteen of 'em. I went fishin' and caught six fish."

"What kind?"

"Minners. Mommy, they had this little girl, she's so little, got little eyes like marbles and a head like a ball!"

"That's a doll you're talkin' about?"

"No! That's a real lady! I saw her pull up her socks! Mommy, you can live out there. I had a job. I got a dollar-fifty, and I found a dollar in the dryer. They don't have so many killings. Only thing that happen there is heart attacks. Or they get bit by sump'm."

"You had a good time?"

"Only one person I can't get along with—I forget his name. He threw the cat on me and I started cryin'. I was gonna hit my head against the electric fence! Ma, why don't you live out there? You got everything you want. You can have a cow."

"Did you learn anything while you were gone?"

"A joke. You wanna hear? A smart boy and a dumb boy was in this store . . ."